WALKING IN HEAVENLY AUTHORITY

Dr. Michael A. Shine, JD, M.B.A, LSSGB.

Gotham Books

30 N Gould St.
Ste. 20820, Sheridan, WY 82801
https://gothambooksinc.com/

Phone: 1 (307) 464-7800

© 2024 *Dr. Michael A. Shine, JD, M.B.A, LSSGB*. All rights reserved.

No part of this book may be reproduced, stored in a retrieval system, or transmitted by any means without the written permission of the author.

Published by Gotham Books (November 22, 2024)

ISBN: 979-8-3305-8413-0 (H)
ISBN: 979-8-3305-8411-6 (P)
ISBN: 979-8-3305-8412-3 (E)

Because of the dynamic nature of the Internet, any web addresses or links contained in this book may have changed since publication and may no longer be valid.

The views expressed in this work are solely those of the author and do not necessarily reflect the views of the publisher, and the publisher hereby disclaims any responsibility for them.

TABLE OF CONTENTS

Acknowledgments iv
Foreword vi
Introduction viii
Chapter 1: What Is Authority? 1
Chapter 2: Dominated Authority 4
Chapter 3: Impatient Authority 9
Chapter 4: Willed Authority 17
Chapter 5: In the Name of Jesus 25

Section Two: Recognizing Your Authority

Chapter 6: Moving Beyond Salvation 33
Chapter 7: Learn How to Walk 42
Chapter 8: Building the Confidence of the Believer 50
Chapter 9: Who Are You? 62
Chapter 10: Get Up and Accept Your Authority 91

Section Three: Utilizing Your Authority

Chapter 11: Using Your Authority Over Intimidation 99
Chapter 12: Using the Authority of the Blood 108
Chapter 13: Using the Word of Your Testimony 113
Chapter 14: Using Authority Over Criticism 122
Chapter 15: Authoritative Weapons 129
Chapter 16: The Authority of Prayer 144
Final Note 155
Bibliography 157
Biographical Sketch of Michael A. Shine, MBA 158

Acknowledgments

As time passed by since 1996, when I wrote this book, I had to really go back and recall all that has happened to me and the people that have impacted my life. Although, I cannot mention all of them by name, I will go ahead and say thanks to all my friends and family before I get started. I want to first dedicate this book to my Lord and Savior, Jesus Christ, who has always been there for me. The book is especially dedicated in memory of my father who passed to be with the Lord on January 15, 2010. He taught me the value of work and how to make the best of what you have and not complain about the outcome. I am truly grateful for his memory and legacy. To my Mother, Odessa Shine, who I live dearly and who taught me how to fight… (I laugh as I write this part). She gave me the inspiration not to give up or let anyone take advantage of me. She and my Dad both taught me in the way of Christ and about His unfailing love. Thanks Mom and Dad.

Thanks to all my sisters (Marion, Wanda, Cynthia, Linda, and Angela) and my brother, Patrick, who were all there with me through the good times and bad. You are all special to me and I never could have gone through the tough times without you. I also wanted to mention my friends at City Hall. You know who you are. I love all of you.

I wanted to thank my adopted sister in Christ, Mattie Akins, for your love and for always giving me materials to read and study. You and your family have always encouraged me. My life has been made better because of you. I do remember I am in the Lord's care. I would be remiss if I did not give credit to my dad in the ministry, Pastor Clyde

Beverly, Sr. who taught me the importance of words and gave birth to me in the preaching ministry. You are such a ray of light and knowledge. I will never forget you. I want to thank my current pastor, Anthony Xavier Page (Face2Face Worship Center)—who allows me to utilize my gifts in ministry and encourages me to keep striving—as well as the members of Agape Baptist. Again, I am thankful to all my friends and family for your love and encouragement. The best is yet to come for all of us.

FOREWORD

According to Ephesians 2:6, believers in Christ have been given the privilege to "sit in heavenly places in Christ Jesus." This description of the believer's position in Christ is what Dr. Michael Shine so masterfully explains in this engaging manuscript - "Walking in Heavenly Authority." This authority comes from the power of Christ, who conquered sin and death through his death and resurrection. Prepare to take a deep dive into understanding the ramifications of your identity in Christ Jesus. I submit to you, that the more you get to know Jesus, the more you will know yourself and identify areas of your life where you can begin walking in heavenly places.

Many books have been written about the authority of the believer, but few have successfully, and in familiar language chronicled the application of this heavenly authority. Dr. Michael A. Shine teaches us "the how" of walking in heavenly places. In his conversational style of writing, he helps us to understand the power of authority, and the importance of moving beyond our salvation to a place of maturity as seen in how we walk, live above criticism, and overcome low self-esteem; which is revealed as a few of the weapons used to challenge the believer's position in Christ.

You are invited to embark on a deep exploration of the heavenly authority bestowed upon us. Through the forthcoming words, you will unearth spiritual truths and wisdom that will illuminate your path to fully embrace this divine gift of authority from God. This book stands as a testament to the boundless grace and guidance accessible to us, empowering and uplifting us to confidently walk in the authority bestowed upon us by Christ.

I encourage you to open your heart and mind to the transformative power of this message, and may you be inspired to embrace your God-given authority with purpose and unwavering conviction.

Get ready to grow, go, and "walk in your heavenly authority!"

Anthony X. Page,

Lead Pastor, Face2Face Worship Center

Introduction

There is a strange paradox about this book—it is not for everyone. It is only for those individuals who want a closer relationship with God. This book serves as an inspiration to equip believers in the walk of faith. It also causes us to recognize the place where God has set us. I feel it is the season for all believers to Walk in Heavenly Authority. The Bible teaches us that there is a time and place for all things (Ecclesiastes 3:1-8). Yes, saints, this is that time. Satan is using all the instruments that he has to exercise his authority over believers. We must know beyond any doubt that we are victorious by the blood of Jesus.

Knowing what authority is in the biblical sense of the word is important for all saints. Many believers have been robbed, molested, and stripped of authority because of a lack of knowledge. My desire for you, the reader, is to learn to partake of the feast that God has laid before you and to exercise the gift that God has given you. Hopefully and prayerfully, this book will help you rise above the standard of mediocrity and reach a level of maturity in Christ. Apostle Paul lets us know in Ephesians 1:3-14 and 2:6, that we are special in the eyesight of God and because of our royal status, He sets or positions us in heavenly places. This is good news. God thought enough of us to place us in the position where He sits.

To fully understand what Walking in Heavenly Authority really is, I feel that embarking upon a study is important for us.

We will examine the aforementioned Scriptures and the theme a bit closer.

The word heavenly or heavenliest implies that the believer's spiritual experience has been identified with Christ in nature (2 Peter 1:4). That is to say that we have life (Colossians 3:4; 1 John 5:12), relationship (Hebrews 2:1); service (Matthew 28:19-20); suffering (I Timothy 3:12), inheritance (Romans 8:16-17); and future glory in the kingdom (Romans 8:18-21). We share these things in common with Christ. Moreover, these are prerequisites for sharing in heavenly authority. Although the Scripture implies that these are heavenly qualities, it does not mean that we have to wait until we get to heaven to share in these blessings. We can enjoy some of them right now!

We are heavenly beings. Since we have the Holy Spirit dwelling within us, our lives are now supposed to be dictated by the Holy Spirit. Although flesh is present, we can still use the treasures afforded to us because of our heavenly transition. Paul also listed these qualities in detail in Ephesians 1:3-14. He proceeds to inform the believer that he or she has now been blessed with all spiritual blessings in heavenly places. We now have been chosen, predestined, adopted, redeemed, forgiven, granted access to the mysteries of His will, inheritance, and sealed by the Holy Spirit. This is a wonderful thing to know; God thought enough of us to include us in the beloved.

Along with the word *heavenly* from a Scriptural point of view, is the word *sit* (Ephesians 2:6). Sit or Seated, when viewed from the Greek translation, implies that one has been placed in a state of rest or in a reclined position. This does not water down the message that we are conveying. Yet, it does imply that God has seated us in a position of power. Thus, the definition of authority is birthed. In the aforementioned Scripture, Ephesians 2:6 from the Amplified Bible gives a great descriptive view of heavenly authority. It states, "And He raised us together with Him and made us sit down together [giving us joint seating with Him] in the heavenly sphere [by virtue of our being] in Christ Jesus (the Messiah, the Anointed One)."

This Scripture and other prior words crystallize the theme of the book and shed some light on what walking in heavenly authority really is.

We must not fail to mention another key word noted in the theme or title of the book that is, walking. Walking does not imply the physical use of the legs to get to a particular location. When we view this word from the spiritual perspective, it carries the weight of one's life-style rooted in Christ. Vines Expository Dictionary states that the walk is "signifying the whole round of activities of the individual life, whether of the unregenerate [Eph. 4:17-19] or of the believer [Col. 2: 6]. Furthermore, this word is not presenting the view of a temporary walk, but an everlasting one.

Finally, when we consider these words, we can now gain a thorough understanding of why the title of Walking in Heavenly Authority was chosen. I do believe that there is a deeper anointing when we recognize the rights and privileges afforded to us as believers. I am also aware that the devil does not want us to become aware of the powerful nuggets that God has invested in us. When the Holy Spirit reveals this knowledge, it unlocks the truth of whom we really are and who our God is. I declare as you read this book, your life will change miraculously to the point that it will be contagious when around others. You are special. You are in the majority in Christ! So, therefore, gird up your loins and walk with dignity, for God's banner will be forever raised, especially, when you are walking in heavenly authority.

- Rev. Michael Anthony Shine, MBA

Chapter 1

What Is Authority?

Genesis 1:28

Authority, as we know, has been transformed in the arena of worldliness. Humanity has taken their little ability or finite knowledge and used it for their own manipulation. They have used it for self-glorification, status, or even a greater degree of independence. This has constituted a falling away of mankind from the spiritual state with our Heavenly Father into the worldly arena of sin with the devil.

Authority in its purest and most spiritual nature was never intended to be used negatively. It was set up to uphold the standards of God and designed to complement the creation of the world. The meaning of authority from a biblical point of view can be expressed as "God's directed actions delegated exclusively to man." Many people often use the word authority for the word power. Although these words can be used interchangeably, there is a difference. Power means that a person is endowed with the ability to do a specific work, or to exert force upon a task. The Greek word for power is "dunamis" (dynamite), meaning potency. Given this definition, many people can have power or plenty of ability, but they do not have the backing of a higher official. This is the difference. Those who are in Christ have His authority and power. Often, we do not understand how to use it. Many believers are embracing the world's view of authority to cloud their judgment of how God's work and instruction of His people should be carried out. The world says that one should be dogmatic or harsh. Others say that we should use our positional weight to get what we want out of life. In either instance, the world's view of authority is misleading.

We should not be carbon copies of the world, but relatives of heavenly authority. God did not create His sons and daughters to be impacted by the world, but we as powerful believers have an obligation to make an impact upon it.

The definition of authority can be found throughout the Bible and can be seen in God's creation of Adam and Eve. God gave Adam and Eve everything they could possibly imagine, and He also instructed them (or directed their actions) in this process. The Amplified Bible states in Genesis 1:28: "And God blessed them and said to them, be fruitful, multiply, and fill the earth, and subdue it [using all its vast resources in the service of God and man]; and have dominion over the fish of the sea, the birds of the air, and over every living creature that moves upon the earth."

God had blessed Adam and Eve and made them overseers of His creation. Their main purpose was to manage the day-to-day activities of what was created. Adam and Eve did not recognize the great position to which they were elected. They did not know that their positions were of high authority. I believe the failure of not knowing the position where God has placed us can cause great pain. It cripples us from being what God created us to be because we do not realize the importance of our position. It causes us to be ineffective just as it caused them to be ineffective. I am convinced that authority should never be used without the consent of the author. Often we walk outside the parameters God has set for us and we find ourselves in positions that we should not be. This is evident in the fact that God commanded Adam and Eve not to eat of the tree of the knowledge of good and evil for they would die (Genesis 2:17).

Not only was spiritual death an occurrence, Adam and Eve were stripped of their authority. How many of you have been tricked and stripped of your authority by the devil? As he was in that time, he still is. He is using his wicked authority to steal, kill, and destroy (John 10:10). One of my favorite Scriptures that displays the devil's intensity to try and overthrow believers is found in Revelation 12:12. "Therefore rejoice ye heavens, and ye that dwell in them. Woe to the inhabiters of the earth and of the sea! For the devil is come down unto you, having great wrath, because he knoweth that he hath but a short time."

The devil is angry and upset. He is out for the kill and knows that he has a destiny aimed in hell. This should be an alarm for us to take notice that the devil is not playing. John used a strong word "woe", which implies that one should beware of the evil that is about to come.

One thing that I love about God is that He is constantly warning and giving us an opportunity to get prepared to do battle. He allows His majestic wisdom to flow through our minds so that we can arm ourselves against the enemy. God releases or delegates His authority to us so that we can be fit vessels for the kingdom.

The alarm has sounded! Are you listening? Are you alert? The devil is bold and even confident in his authority. We too should exercise our authority and walk in such a way that the devil trembles at our every move. This is spiritual warfare! We are not fighting against some video game or some simulation; this is spiritual reality. Stay on guard and walk worthy of your vocation.

Chapter 2
Dominated Authority

Domination can be a dangerous weapon! This type of authority is a danger when used improperly. Some people find themselves caught up in the so called "I syndrome" since God has endowed them with special honor. The "I syndrome" has manifested itself throughout many centuries and has led to breached fellowship between God and mankind. God told Adam and Eve in Genesis 1:28 to have dominion over the fish of the sea, the birds of the air, and every living creature that moves upon the earth. He did not tell Adam and Eve to bind or enslave His creation. This type of authority places shackles on much of God's creation. From this Scriptural text, having dominion really meant Adam and Eve were to rule God's heritage with wisdom, divine guidance, and, most of all, with respect.

The Bible teaches in I Peter 5:1-3 that we should not be dictators over God's heritage (His people). Instead, as the Amplified Bible states in I Peter 5:3: We should not be "...domineering [as arrogant, dictatorial, and overbearing persons] over those in our charge, but being examples (patterns and models of Christian living) to the flock (the congregation)."

This type of authority is what we do not need. It does not lead to good God-fearing examples.

Godly examples are what we need, and not lords. We can no longer afford to embrace an authority that does not set a positive example. The only example one can learn from this type of authority is that it does not result in any.

I am reminded of a particular verse in Ruth 2:4 that made an indelible impression on my life. As Boaz journeyed from Bethlehem, he saw his employees picking crops in the field and he said, "The Lord be with you." And they answered him, The Lord bless thee." Boaz loved and respected what God had given him. Boaz was not domineering. He knew how to handle those individuals whom God had entrusted in his care. He was gentle with them and they were gentle with him. He knew the right words to say and the appointed time to say it. If we as believers want to be graced with reciprocal blessings in our lives, we must learn how to humble ourselves as did Boaz. We can sometimes dethrone the blessings that God has for our lives if we continue to have the spirit of negative domination.

Negative Domination

Consequently, domination when used negatively leads to destruction, low self-esteem, flawed character, and a lack of motivation. When used positively, it is carried out with wisdom and yields fine character, dignity, and respect for leadership. Believers and all leaders alike should be mindful of the fact that when one is leading, others are affected by their guidance. How are you leading? Is your leading out of negative domination?

I remember working for a lady who was very dictatorial. Everything she did caused me strife. She would not ask me in a gentle way to perform a task. It was always in a demanding manner. "Michael, get this, do that…" and not a measure of kindness was voiced. Many of the people around her were so bothered by her domination that they could not even stomach her presence.

I later learned that this is how negative domination works. It constantly wars for control. It always desires attention and allegiance.

Negative domination is a spirit dispatched and devised by the devil. He knows exactly how to pressure and perplex you. Just like the lady whom I worked for; the devil is constantly devising plans to snuff you out. The devil can get into the mind of an individual to use deceit and lies and to go as far as to back you into a wall where there seems to be no escape. He will try to make things appear as if they are advantageous when the whole ploy is to deceive. The enemy knows how to exercise this area in a mighty way. Nevertheless, we must learn how to counteract his tactics with God's Word.

Overcoming Negative Domination

Jesus displayed the greatest tactic when He counteracted the devil. The enemy wanted to express his authority over Jesus at his lowest state (Matthew 4:1-11). He knew Jesus was down, tired and hungry, and had a great mission ahead of Him, but he still tempted Jesus. So it is with us! The devil will catch you at your lowest moment to carry out his plan. As a lion studies a deer or a lamb to figure out its weak spot, so it is with the devil. He studies you. He tries to filter you. He tries to decrease your faith and then steps in for the kill. Yet, we as saints have an arsenal against the enemy, and it is the same weapon Jesus used—the *Word of God*.

However, do not let negative domination drive you away from what God has designed you to be. He has uniquely crafted and constructed you to be equipped with His power. He tells us in 2 Corinthians 4:7, we have a treasure in these earthen vessels and that the excellency is of God. In other words, we have the Holy Ghost. The Holy Ghost serves as our protector against all evil the enemy dispatches. We are not in control of ourselves; it is of God. We are not able to fight the devil by means of our flesh. Flesh cannot fight against evil spirits. We must always remember that we cannot fight a spiritual war with physical means. The Holy Spirit will fight for us.

After I was exposed to the attacks of my boss for a period of time, God instructed me to simply have a conference with her in a humble, yet authoritative manner. As we talked, I kindly asked her if she would stop her attacks. She stated that she was unaware that she was doing these things. After a span of a week, I could really tell that there was a difference in the work environment. She was more conscious of her mannerism and it changed what others thought about her. Furthermore, when a person presents himself as dominating or overbearing, the thing that the believer has to keep foremost in mind is that we are not fighting against the person, but the evil in the person. When we keep this in perspective, then we prevail.

Humble Yourselves

God has revealed a mind boggling point to me and many people cannot understand it: "If you really want the authority of God, learn how to humble yourself in Him. For in due time you will be exalted" (I Peter 5:6). You do not have to use force to be dominant or to make your presence known. God will look upon your humbleness and place you where you need to be.

Although humility is looked upon as a weakness in the world's eyesight, God looks at it as a strength. Just because a believer is humble does not mean that he or she cannot be dominant. It does not mean that one should allow people to mistreat them or overpower them. What it does mean is that a person knows when to exercise wisdom over a matter and at the appropriate time. The flesh has a tendency to cry out or want to fight back when it encounters opposition. This is only natural. When we become aware of the innate ability to fight, we must constantly use the power of humility to put our flesh back into its proper place. We must remember that one who uses negative domination does not understand the power of humility. So we have an advantage over our enemies. Humble yourself.

Chapter 3
Impatient Authority

As I was arriving back in Birmingham, Alabama from a business trip, God was really speaking to my heart about this portion of the book. He said to me, "An aspect of authority people rarely think of is that of impatience." Many of you might be thinking, 'he has *lost* his mind.' No, this is a type of authority. It can be seen in I Samuel 13:1-14 where Saul was King of Israel and was about to enter battle with the Philistines. Below is part of that Scripture: "And he tarried seven days, according to the set time that Samuel had appointed: but Samuel came not to Gilgal; and the people were scattered from him. And Saul said, Bring hither a burnt-offering to me, and peace offerings. And he offered the burnt-offering. And it came to pass, that as soon as he had made an end of offering the burnt-offering, behold, Samuel came; and Saul went out to meet him, that he might salute him." This was a case of importunity, stress, dire need, and a sense of helplessness. Saul and Jonathan were victorious in a battle against the Philistines, but the Philistines did not take defeat well. They had come to get revenge on Saul because of the victory. The Scripture says that the "Philistines gathered thirty thousand chariots and six thousand horsemen and people as the sand which is on the sea shore in multitude (1 Samuel 13:5)."

In other words, they were outnumbered, and the enemy was armed and dangerous. Saul was looking at the outward appearance or at the immediate circumstance. Many of us are the same way. We look at the current situation and think defeat and try to make amends to counteract suffering. However, God still tells us in dire situations to be still and know that He is God (Psalms 46:10).

Impatience also causes us to be curious. We have all heard the expression "curiosity killed the cat." This is a wise statement. Contrary to this belief, believers should not walk by curiosity, but we have a higher command that "we walk by faith and not by sight" (2 Cor. 5:7). Although Saul was the ruler of Israel and was in authority, he failed to seriously realize that God had given him a command to tarry seven days (symbolic of completion). Nevertheless, Saul was impatient! Saul let his kingly authority detach him from God's heavenly authority. Sometimes our positions, whether secular or religious, sway us to do things outside the sphere of God's will. Many of us should be able to identify with this picture. Much of this is apparently going on in the contemporary church, on our jobs, and even in our homes.

The Scripture states that Saul should have "tarried seven days, according to the set time that Samuel had appointed" (1 Samuel 13:8a). There was a reason for this seven-day period. God knew about the battle against the Philistines and prophetically spoke the seven days appointed time into existence. I do believe that there is an appointed time for believers. Your appointed time may not be like mine, but all of us have appointed times. God sees time as a means of developing character. Our importunity or our being impatient does not move Him, but our faith does. He wants to foster you into the man or woman of God that He would have you to be. We must admit that we have not always followed God's divine guidelines, but in the arena of error, we find ourselves wandering back to God, our longsuffering friend.

Saul, in this Scripture, represents sin collectively. He also is an example of that side of us that is ready to give birth before the time. Saints, sometimes God is telling us that it is not time to give birth. Being pregnant beyond the nine-month period may seem abnormal, but God transcends abnormality. Your nine months may be two, three, or five years, but if you walk upright for that expanded time you will yield a harvest of blessings.

The appointed time was not up. Although it was the seventh day, the end of that seventh day had not yet appeared. God has a strange way of dealing with time. You may have set your schedule for Friday at noon for an important deadline. Eleven-fifty has come around and there is still no sign of hope. At the brink of 11:59, God steps in on time. Many of us are like Saul; noon has not yet come. We are expecting, hoping, anxious, and ready to give in, but our noontime has not yet arrived.

Because of Saul's impatient attitude, he began to offer up a sacrifice to God and act out of his authority. Although he was king, he was not the one to offer up the sacrifice.

When Samuel returned, Saul set out to meet him and saluted him. This scenario is like that of a child who has done wrong and one of his ploys to downplay the action is to retreat to a happier atmosphere. The Bible said Saul went out to meet Samuel (1 Samuel 13:10). In other words, he walked away from the place of error. Many of us walk away and we do not stand to take responsibility. Nevertheless, Saul, outside the damaged area, stood there and made excuses for what he had done. Listen to Saul's response to Samuel.

"And Samuel said. 'What hast thou done?' And Saul said, 'Because I saw that the people were scattered from me, and that thou camest not within the days appointed and that the Philistines gathered themselves together at Michmash; Therefore said I, The Philistines will come down now upon me to Gilgal, and I have not made supplication unto the Lord: I forced myself therefore, and offered a burnt-offering.' And Samuel said to Saul, 'Thou has done foolishly: thou has not kept the commandment of the Lord thy God, which he commanded thee: for now would the Lord have established thy kingdom upon Israel forever. But now thy Kingdom shall not continue: the Lord hath sought him a man after his own heart, and the Lord hath commanded him to be captain over his people, because thou hast not kept that which the Lord commanded thee'" (I Samuel 13:11-14).

Saul began to offer excuses to Samuel for what he had done. He began to look at people, and took his eyes off the one who created the people. Saints, being impatient, will breed excuses. It causes a person to fumble or search for some external reason for a wrong action when the answer lies in the fact that we were just impatient. Do not let people be your reason for walking outside the authority God has given you. Learn to trust and rely on Him who is trust-worthy. As a result of Saul's actions, God rejected him. But even more alarming, he was stripped of his blessings and authority. And God chose someone else to do the job. Can you imagine Saul looking at David saying, "It could have been me." Some of us are in the same position as Saul, but we have been released from our own authority by being disobedient. However, some of us are saying, "that could have been me."

Where do you fit here? There is still a place for you in God. No matter how bad you have messed up or given up, God will take all of your messes and turn them into blessings. He is just that type of God. Think about it!

Wait on God

Waiting may be one of the hardest things to do. We are often so anxious. I have come to realize that anxious attitudes can lead to unthankful gratitudes. If we force ourselves into an area before our season, we will not enjoy it as much as we would if we had waited.

Waiting implies some duration. God does not often reveal his time, but what He does tell us is simply to wait. While we are waiting, we should have a servant mentality. We should not allow ourselves to stop rendering service to God because we are in a holding pattern. I can remember the depression that I suffered on my job. I was twenty-four years old and on the verge of being fired for standing up for what was right. Depression had set in and my whole life seemed to be in shambles. I did not understand why God would tell me to wait when I was so depressed. I knew that I loved Him and He loved me, but why the two-year wait?

While in prayer, God instructed me to praise Him while He was preparing the blessing for me. He told me that if I praised Him now, I would reap a blessing later. I had to learn the power of serving God in my personal waiting room.

At the time, it seemed lonely and dreary, but at the end, I saw blessings of sunlight. I declare to you to serve God while waiting. If you serve Him or wait on Him now, you will increase a storehouse of blessings later.

I have often heard people quote the Scripture, "weeping may endure for a night but joy cometh in the morning" (Psalms 30:5), and I think that we sometimes set ourselves up for a fall. We say that weeping may endure for a night, but we forget the three-letter word "may". The mays in our life are so important. May implies that it can probably take a night or it can possibly take two years. Remember my "may" took two years. This exposition of the word is not meant to water down your perception of waiting to be blessed, but it does convey the reality of waiting. Waiting has so many benefits. I did not know about the benefits while I was waiting for God to move. Saul apparently did not either. While we are waiting, we need to sit back and write out in our minds a cost/benefit analysis.

Benefits of Waiting

Each of us can enjoy the benefits of waiting. However, knowing the benefits are important before we can enjoy them. Isaiah 40:31 says: "But they that wait upon the Lord shall renew their strength; they shall mount up with wings as eagles; they shall run, and not be weary; and they shall walk, and not faint."

Benefit One: Renewed Strength

There is a part of the believer that can become stagnant while waiting. We have a tendency to lose our enthusiasm while enduring suffering. We can become low in spirit and we may need a touch from God to revive us. God knows that waiting can take its toll on us, so He will give us a double portion of spiritual energy. He will allow His anointing to overtake us. The anointing will be our spiritual vitamin. God will give us everything that we need to preserve and strengthen us, for His strength is made perfect in weakness. God will cause our strength to be complete in difficult times. It makes a difference when we are waiting on the Lord and not man. The Lord is the only one capable of making our strength new. This is a benefit in that humans cannot renew strength, for the Scripture informs us that "In him, we live, move, and have our being" (Acts 17:28).

Benefit Two: Mounting Up

Once the eagle's strength is renewed, he flies to higher heights. Although there are still storms around the eagle, he soars above them, He now is at liberty. We, too, can be at liberty after we wait on God to prepare the proper table for us. This is an added comfort to know that if we keep our eyes focused on God without being impatient, we will reap a harvest of blessings.

Mounting also implies that we have a closer relationship with God during and after our waiting period. Waiting causes us to learn more about God and depend upon His power to deliver. We can then begin to use our waiting periods as examples for future trials. That is to say, "Since God brought me out or blessed me this time, I am convinced He can do it again."

Benefit Three: The Spirit of Endurance

Once our strength is renewed and is elevated to higher heights in Christ, we then receive enduring power. Isaiah 40:31 further states that they shall "run and not be weary; and they shall walk; and not faint." We can continue since we have stood the test of waiting. We can run through a troop and leap over a wall because of the spirit of endurance. The spirit of endurance is simply allowing the Holy Ghost to take control in fainting situations. There is a spiritual pep-up that overtakes us when we allow the Holy Spirit to control us. Overall, this verse serves as a reminder that we have a new zeal and new determination to press on despite circumstances.

As we can see, possessing authority that is impatient leads to ill choices. However, when we wait patiently on God, it leads to choice blessings. Let us learn how to wait.

Chapter 4
Willed Authority

Luke 10:19

We, as children of God, are privileged people. Jesus has given us authority that He has not given any other creature on the face of the earth. He has adopted us into His royal family and esteems us as partakers of His royal authority. As stated earlier, authority was ordained of God from the beginning. Then, why is the Church stagnant? Why are we not exercising the gift that God has given us? I do believe that the stagnation of the church lies in the fact that we do not understand the true meaning of the church nor do we understand the power the church has.

In Luke 10:19-20, Jesus was giving a charge to His 70 new disciples. He declared to them as they journeyed to do the work of the Lord, to take notice of the power that He had given them. He said, "Behold," take hold of yourself, Look, and examine. I have given something that will aid you in doing the work that is at hand. This is not saying Jesus gave them the Holy Spirit, because the Holy Spirit had not indwelt believers at this time. God did not give the indwelling of the Holy Spirit until the Book of Acts (1:8) and (2:1-21). What Jesus is telling us is that He has willed His ability to us as believers to carry out His work just as the Holy Spirit moved upon mighty men in the Old Testament. We have His ability to cast out devils, and walk upon serpents. He was allowing those believers to pave the way for His coming in those same areas (Luke 10:1). We must realize that when something is willed, it is passed down and has been authorized by the originator. All of us at some point in time have heard of or experienced being in a will. Legally speaking, the person who is in the key position has the right to reserve part or equal share of his or her inheritance with another party.

This is the same manner with Jesus. He has granted us the same rights and privileges. And we must acknowledge that He is still the supreme controller and is there backing all of our efforts. This is wonderful to know that the Majestic King has willed us lowly creatures to share in His authority. I am sometimes baffled at the way God chooses to use us. He could have chosen any other creature to will His power to, but He chose you and me. He could have been selfish with His authority and kept it all for Himself, but He shared it with us.

Occupy Till I Come

In the parable of the ten pounds (Luke 19:11-27), Jesus tells of a story in which a nobleman went into a far country to receive a kingdom for himself. He called ten of his bond servants and entrusted them with ten pounds of a day's wages and said unto them, "Occupy till I come." The Amplified Bible states "buy and sell with these while I go and then return."

When the nobleman left the country, he entrusted them with the responsibility of laboring with the tools that he had given his servants. Jesus used a phrase that should change our whole outlook on authority. He says, "Occupy till I come." This does not suggest sitting and remaining idle. He is instructing you and me who are in charge to carry on the work of adding souls to the kingdom of God. You cannot idly sit and help build God's Kingdom. With His willed authority comes willed responsibility. God holds us responsible for not using what He has invested in us.

Many of us as believers love to be in a will, but we do not like to uphold the duties of that will. Remember, we are people of covenant. With God's covenant, we are held liable for the way in which we uphold our side of the bargain.

When the nobleman returned, some servants had made wise investments and others unwise. Saints, we must remember that the nobleman (Jesus) has a day of reckoning or accounting. He will one day view our spiritual balance sheets to see if we did what we were supposed to do. He remembers the authority that he has willed to us and will one day bring to light the question, "Did we balance?"

Although we as believers have power, we do have some limitations. When I speak of limitations, I speak in the manner of the physical realm. For there is no limit in heaven. Many people sometimes take Luke 10:19 in a literal sense. And we find ourselves in a mess. However, when we read the Word of God, we should ask God to place us in a heavenly mindset to prepare us to be blessed by His Word. Some may take this Scripture and say, "Since I have power over snakes and scorpions, I can walk on them and not get bitten." This is not true from a natural point of view. It is highly likely that if you walk across serpents without God's leading, you might get some bites. But if per chance a believer walks or stumbles upon some vicious serpent, I am sure that God's divine protection will step in to aid in the mishap.

I am reminded of the story of Paul in Acts 28:3-6. After being shipwrecked, Paul started to make a fire. He reached down to pick up some sticks and laid them on the fire and a venomous beast hung on his hand and he shook the beast into the fire. He felt no harm.

Paul was not picking up the snake as a ritual; this was a circumstance that tested the power of God. God's power overthrew the enemy in this scenario.

Jesus is not using this Scripture in a literal sense. He is using it figuratively. Jesus has willed His authority to us to have dominion over all evil. Evil in this scripture represents the scorpions and serpents. Whatever the evil: wicked spirits, hatred, negative domination, selfishness, or jealousy, we have power over these devices because of Christ's willed authority.

However, there are many denominations building themselves on Luke 10:19 and Numbers 21:8-9, but I am sad to say that those Scriptures are being taken out of context and require a heavenly mindset for the correct interpretation.

Delegated Authority

We can also view willed authority as delegated authority. They can be used interchangeably. We usually use delegated authority when we refer to a physical work environment, but this can also be used in the spiritual realm.

As stated earlier, when we delegate authority the one who is the originator or the holder of the will passes it down. Even from the spiritual standpoint, God has delegated His authority to us. We are delegates for God. We are here to act on His behalf. He has favored us and that seals us with heavenly backing.

Even in Scripture, God enacted delegated authority for His early believers. One example is that of Moses and his father-in-law, Jethro (Exodus 18:13-25). Moses, being the leader of the Israelites, began to give counsel to the people from dawn to dusk. Jethro was very displeased with this matter and said "...The thing that thou doest is not good" (Exodus 18:17). Moses' father-in-law was concerned that Moses would tire himself from judging all the cases of the people. He, in turn, instructed Moses to draw out from among them men who stood for truth to aid in judging God's people. These men would hear the smaller cases and bring the larger ones to Moses. This story brings into account the realism of the modern-day church and work environment. We have gotten so accustomed to bringing all of our matters to our pastors, and have failed to realize that pastors have other priorities. However, this is not to say that the pastor cannot hear our concerns, but God has delegated authority to the body of Christ. He has delegated deacons, teachers, counselors, and even strong Christians.

Sometimes we bring all of our pettiness to our pastors or leaders when we could solve the problem ourselves. There should not be room in the body of Christ for pettiness. We should be far above it. If we learn the process of delegation, we can take more pressure and stress off our pastors and make their professions easier.

The Prerequisite for Using Willed (Delegated) Authority

All believers have access to this willed authority. The primary prerequisite for having willed authority is to be in the *Will of God*. You cannot exercise power over the devil if you are not in God's will. The seven sons of Sceva were witnesses to this fact when they tried to cast out devils. It could not be done although they used the name of Jesus (Acts 19:14-18). What is really important for us to remember is that Satan knows who is in the will of God and, most of all, God knows. The spirits knew Paul and Jesus, but did not know the sons of Sceva.

As a result of them not having a relationship with Jesus, some severe actions were taken. We really need to examine ourselves to see if we are in God's will. If we are not, then we need to get into His will by accepting Him as our Lord and Savior. This type of authority rests on the premise of salvation and being adopted into the family of God. God will not give His authority to any person if they do not have a personal relationship with him. I am thankful for being in His will. For being in His will brings many blessings and leads us to enjoy His precious promises.

We Have the Keys

"And upon this rock I will build my church; and the gates of hell shall not prevail against it. And I will give unto thee the keys of the kingdom of heaven; and whatsoever thou shalt bind on earth shall be bound in heaven; and whatsoever thou salt loose on earth shall be loosed in heaven" Matthew 16:18-19.

Have you ever really thought about the importance of keys? Keys play an important role in each of our lives. We need them to open our doors at home or open our car doors. Keys may be used to open up a secret chest that someone may have stored. Given these examples, we see that without the use of a key, some part of our lives would be inoperable.

So it is with the spiritual. Christ has given us the keys to the kingdom of heaven. These are not physical keys. These are keys used to unlock things and issues by relying on the power of the Holy Spirit. Prior to Matthew 16:18-19, Christ was asking His disciples who did men say that he was (Matthew 16:13). Later, Peter spoke by revelation from God, saying that He was the Christ, the Son of the living God (Matthew 16:17). Christ was trying to get an open confession from the disciples so that they would be aware of who they would be representing.

Christ then proceeded to say that He would build His church and establish it based upon His name and His principles. Furthermore, no one would be able to overthrow it. Christ, in essence, is exerting His authority, He is informing us that He has power to keep that which He has established. That is, we as the people of God, are the true church and are called out and eternally secured by the power of His name.

With the authority that Christ exerts, He then leaves or delegates authority to us. He says in Matthew 16:19, "I will give you the keys to the Kingdom." These keys in this Scriptural reference represent a badge of power or authority from Christ. Just as a policeman or an officer wears a badge, you and I also are heirs of a spiritual badge. With this badge comes duties such as binding of evil spirits, casting out devils, breaking bondages, and after the binding comes loosing or releasing a clean environment.

Simply stated, binding and loosing are primarily setting heaven in agreement with whatever is on our hearts that needs cutting away or needs to be set free. When we use this authority, it allows us to enter a covenant with heaven that the things we pray about will happen.

Speaking of prayer, it is one of the main authoritative keys that we can use when we display our Christian authority. Prayer is only one key, but there are many others. Some may use the power of praise or the power of worship. Others may use the power of reciting Scriptures or the power of rebuke. Whatever the case may be, they are all keys that heaven honors.

Furthermore, the keys to the kingdom have only been delegated to the church. No other power has the authority that we have. The carnal-minded man cannot use these keys because he has not identified with Christ's spiritual nature. This is the secret to using the keys to the kingdom of heaven. Let us remember our badge!

Chapter 5
In the Name of Jesus

What is in a name and why are names so important? Names identify our very being: who we are, our purpose, and our character. We have all heard the expression "In the name of Jesus" in some form or fashion. What does it mean? Why is it so important to the believer? First, we should mention that this is not just an expression for the believer. These are anointed words. Many people often use "In the name of Jesus" in joking, jesting, or casual conversation. But I do believe that these "Holy Words" should not be taken lightly. They should be used in direct ownership by God's called - His Church. No other people or agency should have the authority to exercise this power but those who belong to Him. "In the name of Jesus" is special in that Jesus authorizes us to act on His behalf. It also implies that nothing can be done unless we sign His name.

All of us should have been taught that we should sign His name to our prayers. Why is this necessary? The Scripture teaches us that there is only one name that Heaven places high honor upon and that is, Jesus (Acts 4:12). Jesus himself told His disciples in John 14:14-15 that "Whatsoever ye shall ask in my name, that will I do, that the Father maybe glorified in the Son. If ye shall ask anything In the Name of Jesus in my name, I will do it." All Jesus is saying, as my old pastor so adamantly states it, "Jesus has given all His believers a blank check and whatever you need, just write it in and sign it in the name of Jesus."

However, many of us as believers are left lacking because we fail to write in exactly what we want and desire. After all, Jesus said to ask in His name and we have to believe the one who has the final say.

Jesus was and is so serious regarding this Scripture that He repeats the words, "That will 1 do" or "I will do it." Anytime Jesus repeats Himself, it strongly suggests that He means business. This also expresses Jesus' covenant relationship with us as believers. Notice, He says in John 14:13-14, that "I will." This implies covenant and promise. He did not say "I might." It will be done. We do not serve a God who is uncertain about what He speaks. When He speaks, it is assured and done with confidence. That is exactly the way we as believers need to speak. When we say, "I command thee in the name of Jesus to be gone," we should expect some results without doubting.

Doubt is a weapon the devil uses on believers to sift the Word of the Lord from out of our hearts. He wants every baptized, born again believer to nullify or change their words, but we need to be planted, rooted, and grounded and say with conviction, "I take control over all doubt that Satan is trying to use against me to hinder my blessing." Just wait and see, God will move on your behalf.

As a result of Jesus teaching the early followers to ask in His name, many situations and circumstances changed dramatically. One Scripture that is fresh in memory is that of Paul being bombarded by a spirit of divination (Acts 16: 16-24). This young girl was a soothsayer or what we would call a fortune teller. She was in the business of making money for her owners. She followed Paul and Silas many days, saying, "These men are servants of the most-high God." The evil spirit recognized Paul and Silas and began to grieve Paul. Paul, under the unction of the Holy Ghost, turned and said, "I command thee in the name of Jesus Christ to come out of her." And it was done.

One Sunday morning, as I was teaching Sunday school, one of the students interrupted me and said I had a phone call. I rushed to the telephone hoping nothing was wrong with a member of my family. As I picked up the phone, I heard a lady's voice that said, "Get your Bible and turn to the Gospel of John." By this time, I knew who she was. It was a lady who had constantly antagonized our church under a demonic influence. After she stopped reading, she said, "Lucifer is equal with God," and I quickly recognized that the woman was oppressed by the devil with several strange voices emerging, God quickened my spirit to say to her (the demon oppressing her), "I rebuke you in the name of Jesus and Satan you are a liar." After this was done, she began screaming and quickly hung up the phone.

One thing the enemy recognizes is a child of God. He tries everything in his power to grieve us. But by the authority vested in us, we have power over evil spirits. It is not by chance that the enemy stumbles upon believers. He knows exactly who can do damage to his kingdom.

We should also mention that just because a person uses the phrase "in the name of Jesus" to speak healing over finances, health, and extreme situations does not mean that God will allow it to happen. He told Paul in 2 Corinthians 12:9 after Paul asked Him three times to remove his thorn, "My grace is sufficient for thee: for my strength is made perfect in weakness." This lets us know that God does not always remove our thorns. Instead, He uses our infirmities to build character. He looks at the long-term picture while we view the now. We must also understand that "Our times are in His hands" (Psalms 31:15). Although we have prayed in the name of Jesus, God sometimes allows His permissive and divine will to override our wills. I'm sure many of us have prayed, laid hands on, and even signed our petitions with the name of Jesus, and wondered why the person was not healed. It is because all of us have an appointed time with destiny. None of us can change the way God decides to deal with a critical moment in our lives. Sometimes God uses the things that we try to cast out to move the person to another realm of glory.

I am not saying that this is the case for every individual. Some are not healed because of their own lack of faith. When people came to Jesus to be delivered, He said it was so because "Thy faith has made thee whole." So do not get discouraged when a situation turns out in the opposite way. God had and has a better way. Do not allow the devil to condemn you or cause you to be uncomfortable in using those "holy words." Continue to expect things to happen in your life and in the lives of people. Rest assured that God can and will honor our request by His own standards.

Moreover, "In the name of Jesus" should not be viewed as mere words. They activate the Holy Ghost to do battle for you and me. We have no power in ourselves. All power is of God. When we stand together in unity, binding Satan, we release God to do battle or make a remarkable change in our lives.

As we notice in Acts 2:37-41, Peter was a changed man after the Holy Ghost had indwelt him. He began to preach the gospel to men and women of Israel. He began to walk in his rightful position and was speaking for Christ. He learned how to exercise his authority by being bold in whom he believed. He stated that people must "Repent, and be baptized every one of them in the name of Jesus for the remission of sins, and they would receive the gift of the Holy Ghost." As a result of his standing bold in Jesus' name, three thousand souls were added to the body of Christ.

If you want to see a mighty move of God in your life, learn how to walk boldly in Christ. Learn how to get out of your own personality and get into the personality of God. You will never see your family delivered or bondages broken unless you act and walk in the name of Jesus.

Now, what is His name? His name is Jesus and He is exalted above every name. His name means salvation. He is the strong breasted one. He is one that is mighty in battle. He was in the beginning of time and will be in the end. His name transcends our history and all time factors. He is above principalities. He is above fame and wealth and He is more precious than fine gold. He is the Lily of the Valley and the Bright and Morning Star. He is Alpha and Omega, the beginning and the end. And He is most of all, the conquering King, our Savior and Lord Jesus, the Christ!

Section Two

Recognizing Your Authority

Chapter 6
Moving Beyond Salvation

Hebrews 6:1-12

One Sunday, at the 11:00 a.m. service, after the preaching of the message, Jill gave her life to Christ. She walked to the front of the church and extended her right hand to the pastor and in turn, was accepted into the local fellowship. After a span of a month, Jill was only seen twice during the 11:00 worship service.

What happened to Jill? Did she have some unfortunate circumstance? Jill was later contacted and she stated that she had some working conflicts on Sundays. What about weekday services? Jill viewed those days as time devoted to herself. She believed she was saved and did not need all those training sessions. In other words, Jill got the primary part, but was not eager to move to a higher level in God. The above scenario is all too common in the body of Christ. Many believers are just satisfied with salvation and not concerned about building upon what they have already received. I am a firm believer that Christ wants to take us above the call of salvation. Some of you might be saying, "This is what our main focus is. So, you need to leave it alone." The Bible teaches us that we are our brother's keeper and we should do good, especially to those who are in the household of faith. This is why I must inform you that moving beyond salvation is serious business. If we do not move, we are prime candidates to fall back into the world system.

When I speak of moving beyond salvation, I speak in the manner of learning more about Christ. Salvation in its simplest definition is being redeemed from the enemy, that is, being saved by Jesus who freed us from the law of sin and death.

Salvation also has a deeper meaning. It goes far beyond being saved by Jesus Christ. It is the continuation of being saved. Being saved by Jesus is only the beginning point. We need to be constantly and daily saved from things that we associate ourselves with.

I was talking to a young lady about salvation and she explained that she does not like to go to Baptist churches because they teach and focus too much on salvation. I began to share with her that we can never escape salvation because it is a daily need. She never fully understood what salvation was really about. All of her life, she thought salvation was just accepting Christ as her Lord and Savior and never went beyond that point.

However, salvation has several meanings. It means to be healed, saved, transformed, and delivered. So you see, we can never escape salvation, but we can learn more about what salvation can do for us. Moreover, we as saints need to know how to live a victorious life on earth. Satan will try to use all his weapons to gain victory over us. I remember a book that said something to the effect that, "Many people will be in heaven because they truly accepted Jesus as their Savior, but many of these same people will never have walked in victory or enjoyed the good plan God had for their lives because they did not get their mind renewed according to His Word."

There needs to be a constant renewal of our minds. This may involve some deeper study of the Word, burning the midnight oil, and even more time in corporate Bible study. I do believe that many believers have focused their minds so much on the first renewal, that they do not really care about the levels of renewal that come after it. The Bible clearly tells us in Rom. 12:2 "be not conformed to the world, but be ye transformed by the renewing of our minds, that ye may prove what is that good, and acceptable and perfect, will of God." As we notice the "ing" on the word renewing. It is not there just for space. It plays a significant role in how we should perceive this word. It means that there is a continuation of renewal. It does not stop at the point at which we accept Christ as our personal Savior. That is only the beginning.

If we truly want to walk in victory on this side, then it is time to dust the cobwebs off our Bibles and dig into the Word of God, and to see what God has in store for our lives. You will never know what God has promised for your life unless you go beyond saying, "I am saved."

Hebrews 6:1 in the Amplified Bible bears a clear view of moving beyond salvation. It states: Therefore, let us go on and get past the elementary stage in the teachings and doctrine of Christ Messiah), advancing steadily toward the completeness and perfection that belong to spiritual maturity. Let us not again be laying the foundation of repentance and abandonment of dead works (dead formalism) and of the faith [by which you turned] to God, With teachings about purifying, the laying on of hands, the resurrection from the dead, and eternal judgment and punishment. [These are all matters of which you should have been fully aware long, long ago.]

The writer of Hebrews is admonishing us to get past the elementary or basic principles of salvation and move on to greater heights. So many people are in the elementary stage of their Christian development, and should be farther along because of the increased revelations from the Word of God.

Moreover, we have aligned our minds to remain at point A and never get to point B. There should not be any reason a believer cannot move forward in Christ. God wants to promote us in the knowledge of Him. He has laid a foundation and it is up to us to expound upon it. God is not only concerned about the primary. He is also concerned with the secondary. He does not want you to stop at salvation. He delights in seeing you and me moving to new realms of glory. He longs to prosper us into complete spiritual maturity. He loves fostering completeness in us so that we can be a blessing to the body of Christ.

The Amplified Bible uses two strong adjectives in the aforementioned Scripture. It states, "...advancing steadily." It does not say just to advance, but continue to advance. This emphasizes the ongoing acts of us as believers in Christ. Not only should we continue to advance, but this Scripture shows us the pace at which to do so. It tells us to advance steadily. This is a place of habit, one that is regular, consistent, and ceaseless. We cannot stop growing. We cannot be satisfied in the place where we are. I admonish you to press toward higher ground.

Avoid Stagnation

Stagnation can be dangerous. It only causes you and me to become spiritual dwarfs in Christ. Just as the Scripture mentions, we should not turn around or regress to a state God has brought us out of; Instead, "...press toward the mark for the prize of the high calling of God in Christ Jesus" (Philippians 3:14). God has called us to many places, but some have failed to heed His call. He has called us out of dead works, but some are still waddling in them. He has called us from having a condemned mind, but many are failing to hold on to the mind that is in Christ Jesus. The call of God is so vast that we will always be behind if we do not move according to His voice.

Stagnation is merely saying, "I quit, I give up, and I have learned enough." This is a deceptive mind-set. It is progressive to the point of spiritual suicide. When one is stagnant, he or she is saying, "I am in a state of happiness or complacency." Yet, they do not understand that stagnation is an illusion. The devil will make you think that you have reached the apex of your training in God. He will then try and manipulate you into thinking that there is no need for more study of the Word. He wants you to decrease your knowledge of God because it places him in a position to boast of your defeat.

I can remember a time when I became stagnant in the Word of God. I would think that my studying for an upcoming sermon was enough studying for the week. I could only see growth in the preaching area, but other areas in my life were at a standstill. Before I allowed stagnation to take control, I would believe God for greater things to happen in my life, but they would not happen because of my slothfulness. After God arrested my attention to my deficiency, I immediately began to study like I had never done before.

Another side of stagnation is that of laziness. Laziness is the first cousin to stagnation. They are dependent upon each other. Laziness works against the believer's mental and physical state. It causes excuses, boredom, and even spiritual suicide. We, as members of the body of Christ, cannot afford to be lazy. Laziness breeds failure, spiritual dwarfism, simple-mindedness, and loss of self-esteem. Laziness is simply reducing one's ability willingly. If we are going to be who God says we are to be, then we cannot be lazy. Let us rise up and walk.

Better Is Expected

Another point that is noteworthy is found in Hebrews 6:9-10. It states: "But, beloved, we are persuaded better things of you, and things that accompany salvation, though we thus speak. For God is not unrighteous to forget your work and labour of love, which ye have shewed toward his name, in that ye have ministered to the saints, and do minister,"

The writer is of the conviction that better things should be expected from believers. After God has equipped us with the necessary tools to carry on His work, He has a right to expect more. The Scripture lets us know, "To whom much is given much more is required" (Luke 12:48). If He has blessed you with more knowledge of His Word, then you are required to do more.

Hebrews also exposes two unique and important factors that accompany salvation: work and labor. You cannot truly consider yourself a laborer with God if there is no laboring being done. You may be working, but not laboring. Work is simply the ability to do the job under limited constraints, while labor is doing a job by toiling, sweating, and the exhaustion of energy. These are very important in kingdom building and are necessary for personal growth in Christ.

Better does not imply settling. It implies that one has progressed from one extension to the next. There are times in which we need to be discontented when we think things are better. I am reminded that some successes are often brought about through discontentment. Discontentment fosters a measure of desire in us so that we can advance. Every now and then, there should be a spirit of discontent that overshadows us. You may be performing well at your particular craft, but a gnawing thought on the inside of you should make you feel a bit uncomfortable. I am not saying that the spirit of discontentment should cause you to fear, but it should push you to desire a new level.

This may sound contradictory to the Scripture, but it is not. Paul said he was content in whatever state that he would find himself This is not saying that he was all rosy about it. It says that he would not grumble or complain about the situation, but he also knew that he would not remain in that situation. For he realized that he had enough strength in him to overcome the situation through Jesus Christ (Phil. 4:11-13).

This is key for us to remember. Our rite of passage to becoming better is through Jesus Christ. Although education does afford some great privileges, all our growth is by God through Jesus Christ.

Meat Eaters and Milk Drinkers

Finally, Hebrews 5:11-14 uses two items that are essential for growth. They are milk and meat. Both are protein builders for the natural body, and are used as examples of Christian growth. Milk is symbolic of food used for a baby or a babe in Christ. However, meat is used in relation to that of an adult or a mature Christian. God is instructing us from these passages that we have been nursed long enough and we have too many babes in Christ. It is time that we operate on a higher level. This is not saying that a person must become an adult in Christ soon after he or she accepts Him. Nevertheless, he or she should be making some progress.

When a baby is born, he or she has to have some nurturing. The baby is rocked, fed, or given a pacifier to relieve his whining and even given a special crib for its development. So it is with the new believer. The new believer leaves his infancy stage (milk) and maturates to the adult stage in Christ when he begins to feast on the meat of the Word of God. This is the stage which God desires for His children. Moreover, God gets tired with our nursing and says "enough is enough." There comes a time in a believer's life in which he or she does not need special attention like that of a baby. The believer has all the necessary tools to grow on his or her own. I am afraid that some of us have fostered a bunch of milk babies in our churches. We have been feeding them milk for so long that when taught something new, they turn their head in disagreement of the new meat.

The Scripture states that everyone that uses milk is unskillful in the word of righteousness, for he is a babe (Hebrews 5:13). Many of God's people cannot function properly because they have been fed improperly. Some pastors are willfully giving the flock of God "Kool-Aid-and-Jell-O" sermons that cater only to the emotional side of the believer. After these sermons or teachings are brought forth, the flock is left wondering "How should I do this, pastor?" This is a startling state to be in. Although it may seem healthy in the beginning, it is really hurting the believer.

I am reminded of the phrasing that my mother used when she wanted me to eat wholesome food. She would say, "I want you to eat something that will stick to your bones." This is exactly what we as believers need. We need a word from God that will stick to our spiritual bones—a word that will return to our memories when our Christian authority is tested. When we digest this type of nourishment, and then we develop stronger men and women of God.

We, as believers, need to change our spiritual diet. Our eating patterns need to be adjusted. Some have been eating junk-food for so long that they have developed a junk mind mentality. We have been eating off society's talk-show table for so long that it has become a substitute for our Lord's table (the Word).

Even more confusing, we have been substituting televangelism for personal Bible study. I am not discrediting or disapproving of Christian television. It really ministers to me and many others. However, we need to sit down and cut the television off and say sincerely, "Lord, what would you have me digest from your Word today." If we are going to be skillful in the word of the Lord, then we have got to move beyond the milk mentality.

Are you drinking spiritual milk when you should be eating meat? Pick up your Bible and begin to study the Word of God so you can become spiritually stronger. Do not stay in your current state of stagnation, move on to higher heights in Christ.

Chapter 7

Learn How to Walk

Acts 3:1-11

As I was preparing to write this portion of the book, God revealed to me that we have a duty to walk before Him. I was torn as I asked myself, "How can we walk before God when we cannot physically see Him?" God is saying to you and me, "If you want to understand my revealed word, learn how to get out of the fleshly realm and understand me through the Spirit." This is a word from God. Many of us try too hard to understand God by the way we feel. I am sad to say that God is not in the business of dealing with us according to our emotions. The Scripture teaches us that they who worship God must worship Him in spirit and in truth (John 4:24).

Learning to walk is a step-by-step process. You cannot learn it overnight. Just as a newborn babe learns to walk, we should also. We have to go through the stage of crawling before we can walk skillfully in the Word of God. We may wobble or make some mistakes, but we are still learning to walk.

I remember one of my high school teachers who would always stress the need for study and education. He would often give a definition for education and it has stuck with me. He said, "Education is the sum total of life's experiences from birth to death." In other words, we never stop learning. We can also apply this definition to the spiritual side of life. In this Christian walk, there are going to be circumstances we encounter that place us in a position to gain spiritual knowledge. Psalms 23:4 implies that in this Christian walk, we will have some "death-valley" situations. Although we are in the fires of life, we learn from them. That is the reason why the psalmist could say, "It was good for me that I was afflicted; that I might learn thy statutes" (Psalms 119:71).

It may seem like we are not learning anything while we are going through the toughest times in our lives, but we are. The learning may be what some psychologists call "Latent Learning." This view says that a person cannot digest what is being presented to them currently, but in a reasonable period of time, it will be revealed. This is part of the Christian walk. God, through the use of time, has a way bringing to memory why we had to undergo a stressful circumstance.

Walk Habitually

I am reminded of the passage of Scripture where God revealed himself to Abram (Abraham) and said, "I am the almighty God; and live habitually before me and be perfect (blameless, wholehearted, complete). And I will make my covenant (solemn pledge) between me and you and will multiply you exceedingly." (Gen. 17:1-2, Amplified). All God said to Abraham was to walk habitually and be complete. He wanted Abraham to live a life worthy of acceptance to Him so that He could be pleased. One of our main desires should be to please the Lord and make Him proud of us. We should want God to look down and shower His blessings upon us by the way in which we live.

God told Abraham to walk habitually before Him. A habitual walk does not mean a one-day religious meeting with Him, but an everyday fellowship. Our walk with God should be evident in how we speak, live, teach, preach, and share in our daily lives. We should never want to leave his presence for one moment. We should all have a desire to dwell and have sweet communion with Him.

Because of Abraham's upright walk, he was blessed. God sometimes uses strange methods to test our loyalty, but we cannot change His order of operation. If we would just honor His request of obedience, then we, too, can be blessed. I do believe that if we walk uprightly, then we will be blessed.

Walking in God Requires Daily Bread

In Christ is where our sustenance lies. In Him is where our life support is derived. I am mighty afraid that some of us try to live our lives on a day or two's worth of fellowship with Him. Just because we lived right last week does not mean that we have lived right for the rest of eternity. This rule should be effective in our prayer life, street life, and in our quiet time with God. We cannot live our lives solely on what we feasted upon yesterday, we need our daily bread (His Word).

Moreover, our spiritual man is likened to our physical man. The physical man needs maintenance to keep the body up to par. If it is not fed properly, it will begin to suffer from malnutrition. Consequently, if the spiritual man goes neglected, it too will become malnourished. We have to study the Word, eat the Word, meditate and apply the Word to our lives so we can be effective in our day to day dealings. This is why Jesus stressed in the model prayer, "Give us this day our daily bread (Matt. 6:11)." He knew that daily maintenance was needed in this Christian walk.

Walk Like Enoch

One of my friends and I had decided to have lunch and Bible Study. The passage of Scripture that he used was Genesis 5:22, "And Enoch walked with God. He began to expound on this Scripture and proceeded to say that there are days when he did not pick up his Bible to study. Instead, he just "walked like Enoch."

This was a shocking revelation to me to hear a very dear saint of God say that sometimes he did not study. This really puzzled me. I began to say to myself, "There must be some validity to the theory of osmosis."

He further clarified the statements by saying, "Michael, there will come a time when you will just sit and meditate on God's goodness and in turn, become so consumed." This revelation truly helped me. I was always putting myself in condemnation by constantly saying I needed to study. I am not saying that we should not study because the Bible tells us to (2 Timothy 2:15). However, there are times when we need to sit and meditate on the goodness of God. Although Bibles were not printed or written during Enoch's day, God began to reveal to me that you never saw in Scripture where Enoch picked up a Bible or read a portion of Scripture. He just meditated.

Again, I must reemphasize that we must study, but there are also times when God wants us to walk like Enoch. Walking like Enoch does not call for the believer to enroll in a class on meditation, but desires the believer to focus on one thing or several things that God has done and is doing. Meditation is a way of life for the believer. It does not depend upon the amount of knowledge that one has about God, but rather it depends upon how much the individual desires to understand God.

I have come to realize that Christians should not live or walk in straitjackets. We should live our lives free to worship God. Although God does require us to follow his mandates. He still wants us to be free in Him.

Alternate Definitions of Walk

The word walk in Scripture does not only mean living an obedient life to God, it also implies having faith. He tells us that those who are just should live by faith and not by sight. This is one area in which we as Christians fail. We have a tendency to move or navigate based upon what we see. When we approach our life daily with a sight mentality, we mess up and will always rely on the expression, "Seeing is believing." This should not be the motto of the Christian walk. We have a higher goal, and that is faith. You cannot have faith and walk by sight. Hebrews 11:1 declares: "Now faith is the substance of things hoped for and the evidence of things not seen." We cannot apply this definition if we walk by sight.

Another view of learning to walk lies in an implied definition, that is, walking for the Christian is a lifestyle. It is not optional. We should be forever mindful of our walk in life. It implies that we have a standard. We have a degree of finesse. Most of all we do not operate the way the world operates.

I remember while in college, a fraternity had a party on campus and I went under my own will. I knew I had no business being there, but my flesh prevailed. I began to dance provocatively to worldly songs. I did not know that a Christian friend was there. The next day he said to me, "I was not going to get on the dance floor until I saw you dance." This was devastating! I had indirectly influenced someone's life by giving way to the flesh.

This is a lesson to all believers. Someone is watching you. They are watching your mannerisms. They are listening to your words. All of us as believers have indirectly or directly influenced someone's life. Knowingly or unknowingly, we are toying with the salvation of others. It behooves each of us to watch our walk. This is one of the main problems with the Christian church. The world sees how we carry ourselves and does not want to emulate us because of the type of life we are living. This places an even greater burden on preachers of the Gospel and all lay personnel.

How should we walk? According to Romans 8:1, "There is therefore now no condemnation to them which are in Christ Jesus, who walk not after the flesh but after the Spirit." When we walk after the flesh, it places us in a position to be judged based upon what we have done. I declare to you today that if you live by the Holy Spirit, you can have a life full of peace. There is no reason why we cannot live a Spirit-filled life. God is backing our lives with the seal of the Holy Spirit. He is there to lead, guide, and direct us in the way that is prosperous.

As Paul also stated to believers at Rome in Romans 8: 8-9, "So then they that are in the flesh cannot please God. But ye are not in the flesh, but in the Spirit, if so be that the Spirit of God dwell in you. Now if any man have not the Spirit of Christ, he is none of his."

These verses let us know that our walk should not be embedded in sin because it is not our nature. We are spirit beings. Although flesh is prevalent, we should not yield to it. There is something wrong with a so-called believer when the same sin continues to prevail. I cannot say if that person is saved. Individuals may be struggling with an area of their lives and God is the only one that can deliver them out of it. It is not our job to judge whether persons are saved or not. The only thing that we can judge is the fruit of the persons. The fruit shows when individuals are not producing works that are pleasing to God. We cannot live or walk in the flesh and expect God to be pleased. It grieves God when we sin. It saddens Him to see you and me in positions where He, by His Son, delivered us.

Walk in Integrity – Psalm 26:1,3

Our walk should reflect integrity. David wrote in Psalms 26:1, 3, "Judge me, O Lord; for I have walked in mine integrity: I have trusted also in the Lord; therefore I shall not slide. For thy loving-kindness is before mine eyes and I have walked in thy truth."

All David was saying to the Lord was, "I have lived an upright life, one that will represent you well." I wonder how many of us can say that. David was ready for God to try him and put his faithfulness to the test. He knew that his life was not perfect, but it spoke faithfulness and integrity.

Integrity is living a life of fervent trust in God. It implies being genuine or real in God. All God is looking for is someone who is real in Him. He is not concerned about putting on airs to come before Him. He demands realness. He does not care what kind of baggage of sin that you have been drenched in. All He cares about is a vessel that is genuine.

When believers are walking in integrity, they also do not compromise who they are. They do not allow the name of Jesus to suffer loss by reason of their own will. Often we do not understand the measure of weight that we as Christians have. The world is watching our every move.

Some are there viewing our conduct and lifestyle, seeing if we uphold the standards of being called Christians.

Speaking of standards, you and I have an obligation to uphold. Whether we are at the mall or at church, at play or at work, we must keep the standard of God's name high. What type of standards are you keeping? Are they standards that please God?

One thing that I am convicted of is being truthful to myself. Many of us are in denial, and we are not real with ourselves. We allow things to persist in our lives and, when made aware of them, we go into denial. Denial is a dangerous state to be in. It causes persons to lose focus of whom they are and the purpose for their life. Instead, it breeds lies, deceit, and other areas of sin. For I John 1:8 says, "If we say that we have no sin, we deceive ourselves, and the truth is not in us." That is, if we are in denial that we do not sin, then we are leading ourselves astray.

As the old cliché goes, "to thine own self be true." If we consider this self-inventory, we can walk in the authority that God would have for us. Moreover, there is now no need to walk in disgrace, but in integrity.

I want to admonish each of you to recommit your life to Him and for Him. If you feel that you have been struggling with an area of your life, repeat this prayer out loud. "Father, I need you and I am struggling with (insert problem) and I know you can deliver me, for I know that you are the only one that can cleanse me that I may walk the way that you would have me to walk. In Jesus' name, Amen.

Chapter 8

Building the Confidence of the Believer

Joshua 1:5-7

"There shall not any man be able to stand before thee all the days of thy life; as I was with Moses, so I will be with thee; I will not fail thee nor forsake thee. Be strong and of a good courage: for unto this people salt thou divide for an inheritance the land which I sware unto their fathers to give them. Only be thou strong and very courageous, that thou mayest serve to do according to all the law, which Moses my servant commanded thee: turn not from it to the right hand or to the left, that thou mayest prosper whithersoever thou goest." (Joshua 1:5-7). What a powerful Scripture! God knows how to speak a word in its proper season for His people. This Scripture is special in that it speaks right to the heart of the matter.

Moses had died and God had appointed Moses' minister to lead His people to the Promised Land (Canaan). This was a brave undertaking, knowing the report of giants in the land. The Scripture does not say that Joshua needed His confidence built, but I am convinced that God knew exactly what he needed. This goes for any child of God. I know many of us have had things that we were required to undertake. We may have appeared a bit fearful and wondered how we could pursue the conquest. I admonish you to pursue the undertaking with focus and not fear. Fear serves as an antagonizer to confidence. Fear tells confidence "you cannot accomplish the conquest," but confidence can tell fear – "yes, I can!" Confidence means that we are assured in our God and who we are in God. You cannot be confident if you do not know those two key attributes.

We have authority over fear. The Bible tells us that "God did not give us the spirit of fear, but of power, love and a sound mind" (2 Timothy 1:7). We have the ability by activating our faith to command fear to retreat to its commander in chief the devil.

Moreover, we should be confident because our Lord represents confidence. He was so confident in His love that He allowed His only Son to pay the debt that we could not pay. Proverbs 14:26 states, "In the fear of the Lord is strong confidence: and his children shall have a place of refuge." This is refreshing to hear. When we worship and respect our God, we can expect to have confidence. Have you ever worshiped God, and His presence just overwhelmed you? After you left a worship service you felt as if you could take on the world? This is how it should be daily. We should walk in worship so that we can constantly build our confidence. Moreover, you cannot truly overcome the circumstances of life if you are not confident.

I Will Be With You

God made a vow to Joshua as He did with Moses. He promised that He would be with him. These were comforting words to Joshua. It was comforting to know that someone higher than he had the power to watch and take care of him when no other person could. When God speaks a promise over your life, you can rest assured it is done. God has obligated Himself to be there when you need Him.

I am reminded of the scenario when Jesus was about to leave the earth to ascend to His heavenly Father. The disciples were so afraid and comfortless. Their confidence seemed to have drifted away. Jesus, with His soft voice, said unto them, "I will not leave you comfortless: I will come to you" (John 14:18). He is saying the same comforting words to you and me. He will not leave us as orphans without a source of protection. He promised that He would send us another comforter that would guide us into all truth. This comforter is the Holy Ghost.

Sometimes it seems as though He is not there. It appears like He just does not care about our well-being. This is not true of our loving God. It is all in the way we perceive His presence. Perception plays a big part in life.

We sometimes have a tendency to view the duration of our circumstances and think that God is not there. Remember, He is not moved by our circumstances or our importunity, but by our unwavering faith. He has not forgotten you and me. He is there resting on the crest of our heart, saying, "I am with you."

These sweet words are outstanding promises that are sealed in eternity. Just as God spoke them to His servant Joshua, Jesus also spoke them to us. I will be with you.

Confidence Implies Trust

If we would take a moment to analyze the word confidence, we will find that it implies trust. The root word for confidence is confide. Confide has a family of meanings, which are to trust, to believe, and to depend upon. These words are used interchangeably with the word confidence. In short, confidence means to trust. You should not put your confidence in someone you do not trust. This is a very thought provoking point—everyone cannot be trusted. The position of trusting someone is one that has to be earned. We have to search out one's character, know the convictions of the person, and, most of all, observe the way the person views himself. Trust is not designed to be given out casually. It takes time to root and grow.

How does this relate to God and the believer? I do believe that there is a direct correlation. God will never reveal intimate thoughts to a human until that person knows the very essence of who He is. The Bible tells us that the secret of the Lord is with them that fear Him. In other words, this is someone who has a reverential relationship of Him. God is steadily looking for a relationship with man. He wants to reveal deeper truths of who He is if only we develop a close relationship with Him.

I can remember when I revealed some close things to one of my friends. The person made a vow not to disclose any information. Within a matter of days, the information was spread abroad. I was deeply hurt and I vowed not to trust or place confidence in anyone.

This is a familiar scene with a lot of us as believers. It would seem as if believers would have a major degree of trust, but this is not always true. I had to learn that although we can place a degree of trust in mankind, the ultimate trust and promise keeper is God.

I know many of you have been hurt. You may still be in a period of recovery, but God is saying to you as He said to Joshua, "I will be with you." Some of your friends have said that they would not tell anybody. They promised that it was a contract sealed upon love. Nevertheless, they violated trust with infidelity. You feel violated, humiliated, and given to utter panic, but I am here to inform you that, "He will be with you."

Moreover, God is trusting you and me. He is putting a measure of confidence in us to carry out whatever He wants to be done. His heart is saddened when we fail to trust Him. In essence, God is saying "trust me and I will, in turn, perform for you." Will you do it for Him?

I Will Not Fail Thee Nor Forsake Thee

Failure, when viewed from the natural, is possible, but when viewed from the heavenly is impossible. God cannot fail. It is not in His nature to fail. It does not exist in His spiritual fiber. If we are going to be confident in who we are, we must have this planted in our minds that God cannot fail. Many believers are living defeated lives because this view is not settled in their minds. Although one or two circumstances may have taken a turn in the wrong direction, this does not mean that God has failed.

God was speaking this in Joshua 1:7. He wanted Joshua to know that, although the area of leadership to which He called him was a different arena, He would not fail him. There is a simple reason behind this fact and that is: God called and promoted him to this area. Anytime God calls us to do a specific task, we can expect victory. There are times in our individual lives or prospective ministries that it seems as if we have failed. Sometimes we have let our guards down and Satan steps in and knocks us down. He may have won round one, but he has not won the entire war.

God made a promise, "I will not fail thee nor forsake thee." These are His precious words. God does not bear the name of a coward to abandon the promise that He made. He establishes His Word upon His Word. When His Word is spoken, it is guaranteed that it must happen. He is confident in that His Word binds Him to do according to the promise made.

There used to be a time when a person's word counted for something. I remember sitting with an older lady who was very sickly. When she would need some items from the store, she would tell me to call Mr. Lessman at the neighborhood store and tell him to put whatever we needed on her bill. I was always impressed by this process of purchasing merchandise. This was a form of a credit card that was not written in history or financial books. I came to the realization that this is the same way with God. He backs Himself with the things that He stands for. His credit is good. He does not need a promissory note when He is the promisor. He will not renege on His Word.

One night I received a call from a minister friend of mine and he was very upset about church. He said that he had failed in ministry. This bothered me to the point of vexing my spirit. I proceeded to tell him that he is not a failure because, "Only what you do for Christ will last." I knew this was an illusion of the devil. He longs to make you think you are not in God's will. With this thought in mind, we have to learn how to expose the deceit that the devil uses. When we expose deceit, truth abounds. This is one way we learn to use our confidence and walk in the authority that was planned for us.

Moreover, I could identify with this illusion that was being used against my friend. The devil told me the exact thing when I was not getting the compliments on my sermons like other ministers. The devil made me feel insecure. I had to learn to read the Scriptures according to my circumstance and to overcome the antagonizing thoughts. However, God put a particular Scripture in my spirit:

"The steps of a good man are ordered by the Lord, and He delighted in his way. Though he fall, he shall not be utterly cast down. For the Lord upholdeth him with his hand. I have been young, and now am old; yet have I not seen the righteous forsaken, nor his seed begging bread" (Psalms 37:23-24).

This lets me know that, although I may make mistakes or may fall at some point in time, I am not utterly cast down because of my Lord's unwavering hand. I have learned to realize that God honors and orders my steps. Although I may make a wrong turn, He will take my errors and use them as instruments of experience. However, I am happy that God delights in my ways. I do not care what kind of ministry God has given you. You may be a street sweeper for God. If you are walking in the way He has set, then He is delighted.

I remember reading in a book once: "We become a failure when we allow mistakes to take away our ability to learn, give, grow, and try again. We become a failure if we allow our transgressions to activate an internal voice of eternal self-blame and shame. We become a failure if we let the 'shoulds' and the 'if onlys' suck us into their mire. And we are a failure when we become content with failing." What a fitting word in season. (Pause and read it again).

We should not allow one moment in our lives to cause us to wallow in depression, loneliness, or stagnation. God has given us victory by the very words that He has spoken, "I will not leave thee nor fail thee," Do not live in condemnation. Do not allow your so-called failures to override your destiny. You have a place in God and it is not in failure, but in victory.

Be Strong

This is an important area for the believer. Strength enables us to do the work at hand without fainting. We should not look at this area from a carnal side, although the world has blown this area of physical strength out of proportion.

When God tells us to be strong, He is telling us to rely on Him. We cannot overcome life's trials with physical strength. We must trust God. Although we may have money, power, clout, and an abundance of good health, we still do not have the strength that is needed to withstand the attacks of the enemy. It should be mentioned that God does not view strength based on tangible means. He views it from the point of being in Him. He says "Be strong in the Lord and in the power of his might" (Eph. 6:10). Do not allow your strength to be in tangible things, but "in the Lord".

There are still times in my life when I try to handle things with my physical strength. I find myself in an uproar. I become physically drained and my morale becomes low. God begins to let me know that I have been handling things the wrong way. You cannot allow physical strength to take priority over spiritual strength. You will become out of balance.

God not only told Joshua to be strong and courageous, He re-emphasized it so that Joshua would get the message embedded in his heart. He said, "Only be thou strong and very courageous." We must keep this message written in our hearts, minds and spirits. The devil will try everything in his wicked realm to try to sift this Word out of us. He knows when a believer is empowered and full of the Holy Ghost. He then gets upset and tries to intimidate and rule you. It is time for us to put the devil on the run.

The devil has been using his so-called strength to put us on the run. We serve notice to him today that he is already defeated and will not cause us to feel weak in our daily lives. Remember that the devil only gets fuel from us when we do not walk in the strength of God. However, the solution is to be strong in the Lord and in the power of His might. Stay strong!

Assurance of Prospering – Joshua 1:8

I do not believe that I will do a good job. I do not think it will turn out in a positive way. Get rid of these thoughts! You will never move ahead as a believer thinking negative thoughts. There will be a pattern of negativity when you think negatively. Negative thoughts lead to negative acts and then negative results. We should always have the mentality of prospering. We should be confident in knowing that, when walking in the will of God, we will prosper.

Prospering is simply receiving what God has ordained for you and me. Prospering is not only receiving the tangible things, but the spiritual, physical, and emotional blessings. Many people are not prosperous-minded and therefore, prosperity never happens. Many believers only want the physical things from God and ignore the spiritual. This is an Israelite mentality. The children of Israel always wanted something from God and were often disobedient to Him. We must remember that our physical blessings from God are always contingent upon our spiritual relationship with Him. I always refer to Joshua 1:8 when I deal with prosperity because Joshua was a doer of the Word of God. The Scripture says:

"This book of the law shall not depart out of thy mouth; but thou salt meditate therein day and night, that thou mayest observe to do according to all that is written therein: for then thou salt make thy way prosperous, and then thou shall have good success."

This is a powerful Scripture. It is based upon conditions. God told Joshua, "If you do all these things according to what is written in the Word, then you will prosper and have good success." Sometimes we think that God will just bless us because we are His children. This is not always true. God wants to see some action. He delights in us doing His will in His way. God loves busy people in the kingdom, that is, saints that are all about righteous acts.

Many people are busy, but are not busy doing things that uplift the Kingdom of God. We should mention that the keys to prospering in anything we do is obedience and working to build His Kingdom. We need to find ourselves living to please the Lord. And when this is done, prosperity is sure to come. Deuteronomy 28:2 lets us know that when we hearken unto the voice of the Lord, then all these blessings will overtake us. In other words, when we do what is right in the sight of God, we will be blessed beyond compare, for prosperity will come.

Kingdom Seekers or Wealth Seekers

"Therefore take no thought, saying, what shall we eat? Or what shall we drink? Or wherewithal shall we he clothed? (For after all these things do the Gentiles seek) for your heavenly Father knoweth that ye have need of all these things. But seek ye first the kingdom of God, and his righteousness; and all these things shall be added unto you" (Matthew 6:31-33).

This Scripture sets priority over a believer. Jesus calls us to rank the things that are important. He tells us to seek first His kingdom. What is His kingdom? The Kingdom that Jesus is expressing is that of allowing Him to rule over our lives. It is also means being righteous, having joy and peace, all in the Holy Ghost. With His rulership, other things will become secondary. Seek after those things that promote righteousness and truth and God will grant the success that He has for your life.

In contrast to the world's view of prosperity, you do not have to seek after worldly success, promotions, or tangible things. God will add them because of your loyalty to Him and His work. I remember hearing several people say that to get a good job or be in the "in crowd," you have to become a buddy to the leader. This is ill-thinking. God will supply everything that we need. You do not have to seek or become friends with the world to be blessed. If you have a relationship and are walking in the will of God, these things will come. I repeat; you do not have to follow the world, just do the work of God with sincerity.

Consider Your Motives – Haggai 1:5

Some people will do the work of God and are doing it for the reception of blessings. "Let us consider our ways," says the Scripture (Haggai 1:5). 'The book of Haggai is a book of motives. It commands us to consider our ways or the "whys" of doing. When we consider carefully, we begin to think, rationalize, ponder or weigh the pros and cons. We should allow ourselves to do a soul-searching scan to discern if our motives are pure.

Moreover, all of our ways should be considered with a question. Why are we doing the work of God? Is the salvation of others important? What is my overall purpose? Once these questions are asked internally. Then we respond with the right action, and finally our motives become pure. Pure motives lead to genuine acts.

Many people do good deeds because they want prestige, power, influence, clout, and stability. They want to be seen or approved by their peers. Many people live by the motto, "Let me see what I can get out of it." This may seem farfetched, but it is true. What are your motives?

Motives play an important part in our being blessed. I do believe and understand that God knows who is sincere in kingdom building. You cannot get away with robbing God of sincere work. He knows those who want something for nothing. He is aware of false kingdom workers. If you are one of those who is playing at church work, ask God to clean your heart and make your motives pure.

Finally, there is an enlightening word in Psalms 84:1 concerning prosperity. The psalmist declares: "...no good thing will He withhold from them that walk uprightly." This is exciting to know that God honors our walk. He will not hold back from us the things that are rightfully ours. I am assured no one can stop us from receiving good things from God. Although many may try, it cannot happen because God remembers our walk. He does not suffer from spiritual amnesia. He will remember what we do for Him.

So do not get weary when others may be prospering and you are stumbling. Your time is at hand. Too often, we as believers are moved by what others have. We see the material blessings of others and find ourselves coveting those things. Covetousness is not of God. God does not ordain jealousy. Throughout biblical history, we have seen covetousness. The jealousy of Cain, the obsession of David for Bathsheba, the selfishness of Ananias and Sapphira, the trickery of Jacob, and the jealousy of Lucifer for God are all apparent in Bible history. This view of covetousness is not new and has been around since the beginning of the world. I am assured and confident that prosperity will come at an appointed time. Meanwhile, you must remain true to the work and will of God. For He will make your way prosperous.

Chapter 9

Who Are You?

This portion of the book is one that will revolutionize our personality. I do feel that it is very important that we as believers know who we are in Christ. I am confident that God has given me a ministry of informing the Saints of God who they are. This area is a key factor in how we carry out ministry. You cannot effectively minister to people if you are not rooted in who you are. We can cause disaster to ourselves and to the lives of others if we are not completely aware of whom and what we believe.

God let me know that there are so many people who are unstable in their relationship with Him. Because of this, believers allow the devil and other individuals to manipulate them because of their insecurity. Insecurity will rob you of your proper personality. It breeds depression, oppression, and loneliness. It will make you think you are something that you are not. Insecurity will place you in a position of believing every negative thing that someone says about you.

I remember while in college, a young lady had a very unstable personality. She walked around campus seeking affection and love from anyone who would give it to her. She would waltz into the cafeteria and sit with people she did not know. She was very kind, but people would often use and manipulate her. She would take everything people said personally and become outraged. I would often talk with her and share the teachings of Jesus and other good things that would help her. She had already confessed Jesus Christ as her Lord and Savior, but she was still unstable.

One day I received some disturbing news that she was found dead in an apartment complex and it was proven that she had been raped and molested by a convicted killer. I knew she was not safe on her own. The university served as a place of refuge for her, but beyond those boundaries, she was not safe.

What am I trying to convey? We have to be deeply rooted in Jesus. The devil does not only want you to know who you are, but he wants you dead. He will use suicide, peer pressure, persecution, and doubt to try and snuff out your life. Although this may sound drastic, it is true. The devil will use drastic measures to try and take out believers. This is his character. He is malignantly evil, he is vain in his thinking and he exists to steal, kill, and destroy (John 10:10). The devil is confident in his mission. That is the reason why he is so bold. I pray and hope that this chapter and these Scriptures will build your self-esteem and identity.

I Am a Child of God – Romans 8:14-17

After we acknowledge Jesus Christ as our Savior and Lord, We should then claim our rights to the relationship. We are children of God. Everyone cannot wear this title. Many people might say, "God created all of us and that gives us the same rights and privileges." I am saddened to say this is worldly thinking. There is a difference between being people of God and children of God. God created all of us in His image and likeness, but we were estranged from Him after our forefathers sinned in the Garden of Eden. We needed to be regenerated and brought back into the rightful state with God through Jesus Christ. As a result of Jesus sacrificing His life and our accepting Him, made us children of God. Yes, we can all identify with being people of God, but being children of God requires some added work on our part.

Therefore, I am a child of God because I have met the requirement that is, accepting Jesus as my Lord and Savior (Rom. 10:9-10).

Romans 8:14, says, "For as many as are led by the Spirit of God, they are the sons of God." This Scripture implies that the Holy Spirit called us or knocked on our heart's door to be a part of His family. It was not by force that we were led by the Holy Spirit to become sons or children of God, but it was by our own will.

The Holy Spirit will never force a person to do things out of His own will. He gives a person a chance to weigh the options before accepting Him.

A further note is that God is not in the business of slavery or promoting a dictatorial spirit. He does not place negative yokes or bondages on individuals to make them accept Him as their Lord and Savior. He requires that we accept Him willingly.

The word child implies that we have a parent. It gives an indication that a relationship has started and a bond has been made. If we would stop for a moment and look at the concept of our earthly parents, then we can understand our relationship with God better.

Ask Your Father – Mark 11:24

Being a child also implies that we can come to our parents for anything. I know many of you may be saying, "No they cannot come to me for everything. They have got to get out and work and earn money to buy the things they want. I am tired of supporting them." This was partly the sentiment of my parents. I think this is also where we get confused about parenthood. We have always had the mentality that a child wants money. Sometimes that may be the case. But what about love? What about communication? What about comfort? These are the things that we miss. We miss out on being in fellowship with our children because of material thinking.

One of the benefits of being a child of God is that I can come and ask Him for anything (Mark 11:24). A child should not be afraid of asking his parent for anything. One Sunday afternoon, my niece wanted me to go with her to talk with her grandfather about giving her money to get her car fixed. She was very afraid to approach him. I began to explain to her that she should not be afraid to talk with him because of their relationship. Furthermore, she should be able to go to him for anything.

This is the same way with our God. We have the right and privilege to approach the throne and ask Him for anything because of the relationship we now have. There is no need to fear, Romans 8:15 (Amplified) states, "For [the Spirit which] you have now received [is] not a spirit of slavery to put you once more in bondage to fear, but you have received the Spirit of adoption [the Spirit producing son ship] in [the bliss of which we cry, Abba (Father)! Father!" This Scripture informs us that because of the new relationship, we do not have to be fearful or scared to call on our Father. The law, on the other hand, made us fearful. We were in bondage and had no voice to plead our case. But now we have access to come to Him and ask for anything without fear or hesitation because He is our Father.

The Reality of Asking

Just because we are children of God and have rights and privileges, does not mean that we will get everything that we ask for. Let us plant this thought in our spirit. One duty of a parent is to weed out what is bad and keep what is good for the child. This is how God operates for His children. He knows what is best for us and He knows what needs to be weeded out. Do not allow yourself to pout or go into tantrums because God has not given you everything you asked for. He knows what is needed.

An important thing that children need to understand is that they have an obligation to sit and wait until the parent stamps an okay on the matter. This same principle should apply for the child of God. We should not overstep our boundaries when God's okay is not stamped on a matter. We must realize that when this is done, there are consequences to overstepping boundaries. The parent has to invoke punishment. However, God does punish us. He chasteneth those He loves (Heb. 12:6).

We Are Chosen

When I was in elementary school, I remember playing all types of games. A team captain would decide which side we participated on. I always found it fascinating when a good team captain picked me. Although I was not the athletic type, the team captain still chose me. This was a wonderful feeling of being wanted.

This is same way with our God. He is our team captain and He chose you and me to be on His winning team. Despite all of our errors, misunderstandings, and mischievousness, He still wanted us. Being chosen by God is a special honor. It causes us to have pride in our God and in ourselves. Many Christians are still unaware that they are special despite what others think of them.

In I Peter 2:9-10 states, "But ye are a chosen generation, a royal priesthood, an holy nation, a peculiar people; that ye should show forth the praises of him who hath called you out of darkness into his marvelous light. Which in times past were not a people, but are now the people of God: which had not obtained mercy, but now have obtained mercy."

These verses tell me that I am special and no one can tell me that I am not. I know the world has a way of telling you that you are nothing, but we have to learn to believe what God says we are.

If He says that we are chosen, then we are and no one can tell us differently.

People will go as far as to tell you that you will not become anything because your parents were not successful. This is ill thinking. You are royalty. And royalty means that you are among the 'prime pickings' of God's creation.

When I am ministering to people, especially young people, I really focus on this subject of being chosen, because self-perception is extremely important at their ages. What people feel about themselves says a whole lot about what they can become. If people do not think they are special, they will never become special. God says that we are "peculiar" and that says a great deal about our character. The word peculiar means that we are different from the world. We have a different approach to life. It also implies that we are not to compromise who we are. I do believe that chosen people should have a peculiar mindset. Especially, those who are chosen by God.

We should have a different agenda from the world. Our thought pattern should be different. We should not be the type of people who conjure up plans like worldly people as an act of revenge. The Scripture tells us in Romans 12:1, "Be not conformed to this world, but be ye transformed by the renewing of your mind." Saints, this is what chosen people of God should have--a renewed mind. A mind that is free from deceit and malice. If our mind is renewed by the Word of God, then our behavior should be renewed.

Last, but not least, I Peter 2:10 leaves a profound point to be remembered. It says, "Which in time past were not a people, but are now the people of God: which had not obtained mercy, but now have obtained mercy." We were in a lowly state. We had no pride about ourselves, trapped in sin, and we had no outlet. In other words, we had no true identity. We were wandering through life aimlessly without a purpose. Now we have been made a people, that is, a people of God. We now have identity. We now have a purpose. We can now say that we have a true heritage. A heritage that was granted by our Savior's Mercy. Yes! We are chosen.

I Am Forgiven

"[The Father] has delivered and drawn us to Himself out of the control and the dominion of darkness and has transferred us into the kingdom of the Son of His love, in Whom we have our redemption through His blood, [which means] the forgiveness of our sins" (Amplified, Colossians 1:13,14).

Forgiveness is a subject that all believers need to examine. We are sometimes faced with situations that cause us to invoke forgiveness, but sometimes it is left undone. Many times, we as Christians are the hardest people to render forgiveness. But if we would just take a retrospective view on how God did not hold grudges against us, then we would be constrained to forgive others.

Forgiveness implies that there is a change of heart from the person doing the act. When one is forgiven, there is a cutting off of the wrong act and it is not brought up for discussion. Although there may be something there to remind you of what happened, you still should not harp or focus on past wrongs. Forgiveness is not forgiveness if one continues to expound upon the issue. Evidently, the person has made a lip profession, but has not made a heart confession. With forgiveness, there has to be a change of heart.

The aforementioned Scripture tells us that God drew us out of the state we were in and delivered us unto himself (Colossians 1:13). He caused a change of ownership. We were under the slave master of sin. The slave master of sin had such a tight control on us that it caused us to live a life full of darkness. We were liars, cheaters, drug addicts, prostitutes, homosexuals, whoremongers and backbiters. In other words, we were stone-cold sinners. We were slaves to sin.

While I was in college serving as a resident assistant to earn money, I came in contact with a girl named Kelly. Kelly was a very unusual girl. She liked the bang-your-head type of music. One day she came into the building from a party that she had attended the prior night and she did not look her best at all. Part of me did not like her outer appearance anyway, but I admired her intellectual ability. Surprisingly, I came out and told her that she looked like dirt. I felt so bad. She began to cry and that made me feel like I was the lowest man on earth. However, God quickened my spirit to ask her to forgive me. She thought about it for a while and she then forgave me.

I am grateful to God that she and He did not hold that against me. unlike some humans, He allows all the messes that we get ourselves into to be forgiven. He redeemed us (bought us back). How could a majestic God like ours allow His only Son to associate with people who continue to sin? It is because He loved us and still loves us.

It should be mentioned that when one forgives, there should be love involved. It should not just be mere words uttered from the lips, but empowered by the heart. I am convinced that if we love God, we will love our fellow man.

God's love allowed us to benefit from His Son's blood. As a result of Jesus shedding His blood, we were forgiven. The blood of Jesus Christ cleanses us from all sin. This is the type of blood that takes away stains that ordinary blood could not. The Scripture tells us without the shedding of blood, there is no remission of sin (Hebrews 9:22). Blood was necessary in the new covenant as well as the old. When a covenant was signed, it had to be signed and sealed by the blood of an unblemished animal.

Moreover, Jesus is the (New Testament) Lamb whose blood washed away our past, present, and future sins. What Jesus did completed the whole process for the remission of our sins (Hebrews 10:11-13). This is one of the most fantastic things about being saved. We do not have to be slaves to sin anymore. We have forgiveness of our sins. Thanks be to our Lord and Savior Jesus Christ for His unspeakable gift.

No Condemnation – Romans 8:1

Why should a believer live a defeated life? Christ has forgiven us of our sins, and we should not suffer any backlash. Satan will try and bring the same sin back to your remembrance to condemn you.

The Scripture says in Romans 8:1, "THEREFORE, [there is] now no condemnation (no adjudging guilty of wrong) for those who are in Christ Jesus, who live [and] walk not after the dictates of the flesh, but after the dictates of the Spirit" (Amplified).

If we are going to walk in authority, we cannot allow the devil to condemn us for past wrongs for which God has forgiven us. The Word of God says that, "Therefore, there is now…" (Romans 8:1).

One of the keywords in this whole Scripture is now. Now means present day, current, or today.

In times past, we were condemned, but now the story has changed. We must keep this in our hearts and minds.

Even when Satan recalls a sin for which you have been forgiven, you need to respond by saying, 'what sin? I am a new creature, old things (lying, backbiting, etc.) are passed away (buried, dead, done away with) and behold, all things are become new' (life, health, a good mind).

Satan cannot condemn you if you are assured of what and by whom you have been delivered. The only way that he can condemn you is if you allow him.

Nevertheless, Satan will use those individuals close to you to condemn you. He will get into the thoughts of a family member or a best friend to get you off course. They may bring up an incident that happened years ago. This may have been when you were not saved. After those negative comments, then a seed of guilt begins to manifest itself. Do not allow yourself to get weary because of what happened in the past. Do not feel guilty. Guilt is a form of condemnation. It eats away at our spiritual fiber. People will use guilt to manipulate you, but do not be moved by it. Remember, you have been delivered.

Satan uses these devices to cause you to add wrinkles and blood pressure pills to your life. Satan is a liar. Sin shall not have dominion over you (Rom. 6:14). God has already caused you to be victorious. God has caused you and me to walk (or to live) our lives in such a way that the devil and the people he uses are offended at what we now stand for. We now stand for holiness, righteousness, peace and love.

Condemnation is not a part of our nature because we now walk after the Spirit.

There is a strange side to condemnation that we rarely talk about and this is that condemnation does not only come from Satan and others, but what about ourselves?

We can sometimes be so hard on ourselves. We have a tendency to bind ourselves. We wallow in self-pity, depression, loneliness, and we even throw our heads under the covers. For when Christ freed us from condemnation, the whole of us was freed. He does not do a half job in anything that He does. It is always done fully and completely.

We can be our own worst enemy. We allow ourselves to dwell on the past instead of viewing the now. Many times we are primarily concerned about others doing the condemning, but we never really consider how we can condemn ourselves. Apostle Paul had to learn not to condemn himself when others condemned him (I Corinthians. 4:1-5). Consequently, we live our lives deliberating on things for which God has already forgiven us. It is important to know that we are not the ones to condemn ourselves or anyone. The authority to express those powers belongs to God. I think we fail to realize this and it causes us problems later on.

When I have said or done something wrong (as in the situation with Kelly), I have a tendency to soak into "guilt thinking." This is the first impulse of a believer. In essence, I begin to think that I am a bad person. God then reminds me that "today, there is no condemnation to them who are in Christ Jesus." Today is your day. Do not allow your thinking or the devil's thinking to commit you to the domicile of doubt. You may have said something, or done something wrong, but you do not have to wallow in it.

God is saying to us, just as Peter told the lame man sitting at the gate called Beautiful, "Rise up and walk" (Acts 3:6). Rise up and Walk! Throw that cover from off of your head, turn that frown into a smile, start leaping for joy, start praising God for the victory that you already have! Now is the time of your victory. Now is the time to be freed from all doubt because God through Jesus Christ has delivered you and me. You are not condemned!

I Am Justified – Romans 5:1

With the process of forgiveness comes another area of which we as believers should be fully aware. This area is that of justification. We are considered or counted as justified by what Christ did on Calvary. Justification is the act of God through Jesus declaring us righteous from dead works. This is not a separate working of the Holy Spirit. It is a complete package with salvation.

Romans 5:1 states, "Therefore, since we are justified (acquitted, declared righteous, and given a right standing with God) through faith, let us [grasp the fact that we] have [the peace of reconciliation to hold and to enjoy] peace with God through our Lord Jesus Christ (the Messiah, the Anointed One" (Amplified).

Saints, we have been acquitted of what the law condemned us of. We were not capable of following all the laws that were added to the Ten Commandments. Our minds were too fragile to comprehend or perform what the law expected of us. We were acquitted of wrong acts. The word acquitted implies that we have been found innocent of an expressed wrong. The law said that we were guilty, but God said we were innocent in His eyes. God knew that the additional laws that were added to the Ten Commandments were impossible for us to follow. The law was weak through the flesh, so God instituted a plan with His son, Jesus, to come and fulfill the law and also justify us (Rom. 8: 3-4).

Just because God has declared us righteous does not mean that we will always act right. We, as believers, do fall. We are not perfect. We do sin, but we should not be lost in sin. Being right in the eyesight of God is simply doing what He says. It also means that we should have love, do good to our fellow man, and walk in the way that leads to peace. God delights in us following His commands. He smiles when we do right when wrong follows and tempts us.

Although He has declared us righteous, it is up to you and me to accept His righteousness. Righteous living can be obtained. It is not a dream. It can be a reality.

I often tell young people that doing right is not foreign, although the world displays a different view. It is possible. Being declared righteous does not give us license to invoke a spirit of haughtiness. Walking in heavenly authority means that we should learn how to humble ourselves. Just because we are born again believers, we are not held higher than anyone else. God is no respector of persons (Acts 10:34). If we would really align ourselves with the way God views righteousness, we will know that our righteousness is considered filthy rags (Isaiah 64.6). Do not allow yourself to become self-righteous, but put on the righteousness and humility of God.

I Am Sanctified – I Corinthians 6:9-11

When I was younger, I always thought that being sanctified was a cosmetic work. I would often see ladies with their long flowing dresses and Bibles under their arms, and men's ties were neatly tied around their necks. For a long time I thought this was the life of sanctification. Many so-called saints would often say "I am sanctified" or "I go to a sanctified church." This used to belittle me because I grew up in a Baptist church and we never really used the word sanctified in the context that "sanctified people" used it. As a result of my perspective toward others, I began to question my own salvation. Was I saved? Was there something I was missing?

One day I really examined the lifestyle of a young lady who went to a "sanctified church." I noticed that she wore long dresses all the time, and would habitually use the expression "praise the Lord" and "hallelujah." But a paradox came about in the examination. She would often use profanity like that of a sailor and mistreat others. Then I realized that being sanctified had nothing to do with long dresses, neckties, and Bibles under the arms. They were only surface items. They were items that blocked my view of what sanctified really meant.

As I studied the Scriptures, I realized that I was sanctified. The Bible states in I Corinthians 6:9-11, Know ye not that the unrighteous shall not inherit the kingdom of God? Be not deceived: neither fornicators, nor idolaters, nor adulterers, nor effeminate, nor abusers of themselves with mankind. Nor thieves, nor covetous, nor drunkards, nor revilers, nor extortioners, shall inherit the kingdom of God. And such were some of you: but ye are washed, but ye are sanctified, but ye are justified in the name of the Lord Jesus, and by the Spirit of our God."

Those who are sanctified are the ones who have traded their ragged lifestyles for God's lifestyle. Sanctification is simply living a set-apart life from the world. You cannot walk in the authority of God and live a life that is ragged, loose, and overall, worldly. You have to be one that allows his or her life to be an example of our righteous God.

Sanctification is also an inward response to Jesus' outward expression of love. It has to start on the inside of a believer and then becomes apparent on the outside. Too many people think that it starts on the outside with the cosmetics and then manifests itself on the inside. There has to be a change of mind, heart, and spirit. When the inside of persons change, the change affects the whole man. Jesus is not only concerned about part of you. He is concerned about the whole of you. This is the reason the apostle, Paul, told the believers at Rome in Romans 12:1, "I beseech ye therefore brethren by the mercies of God, that ye present your bodies a living sacrifice, holy, acceptable unto God, which is your reasonable service." God desires that the total man (spirit, soul, and body) be used for the glory of God and to be set aside as a holy vessel.

Holiness is a part of sanctification. They are interchangeable. Holiness, just like sanctification, is not a religion or denomination. It is what God called you and me to be. He expects us to be holy. We, as believers, cannot be separated from holiness. It is what and who we are. God told us to be holy for He is holy (Leviticus 20:7).

First Corinthians 6:9-11 also says that we were some of those aforementioned people. We had our conscience sealed with unrighteous behaviors that separated us from God. We were separated from God through lying, backbiting, stealing, etc. Sin was the main ingredient.

Our now separated lives are the result of the washing away of our sins through Jesus' blood. His blood was the only significant issue that could cause sanctification to come into being. In the dispensation of old, many people used the blood of goats, turtle doves, and lambs to sanctify themselves. But New Testament believers are sanctified by blood of The Lamb (Jesus).

Hebrews 9:11-14 states: "But Christ, being come an high priest of good things to come, by a greater and more perfect tabernacle, not made with hands, that is to say, not of this building; Neither by the blood of goats and calves, but by his own blood he entered in once into the holy place, having obtained eternal redemption for us. For if the blood of bulls and of goats, and the ashes of a heifer sprinkling the unclean, sanctifieth to the purifying of the flesh: How much more shall the blood of Christ, who through the eternal Spirit offered himself without spot to God, purge your conscience from dead works to serve the living God?"

Our sanctification came in a more excellent way. We received Sanctification from the blood giver. We did not receive atonement from a created Lamb, but the self-existing One.

Moreover, His sacrificial blood not only sanctified us, but cleared and cleansed our conscience from dead works. We do not have to think wrong thoughts or do wrong things, because the blood of Jesus continues to purge our conscience from dead things.

We as sanctified believers should not have any dealings with dead works. Dead things have a place of association of their own. We should not go and dig things from the grave that God through Jesus Christ has buried. You should not be persons who have spiritual fantasies with dead works. You are living. Leave dead works where they need to be.

We have many believers who are still hanging on to dead things that can cause a deadness in their spirit man. We sometimes hold on to deadbeat friends, dead songs, dead prayer lives, and even more alarming, dead ministries.

In the words of my mother, "If there's anything that is dead, it needs to be buried." If this sounds like you, bury those things. We cannot afford to hang onto things that cause us to focus on the past and tries to hinder the future. If we plan to walk in victory, we have to let deadness go and cleave to sanctification. After all, this is where God has called us.

I Am Blessed – Ephesians 1:1-14

I remember meeting a young lady at the University of Montevallo in Alabama who was a strong Christian. Always in passing, I would ask how she was doing and she would reply that she was blessed. For a long time I thought she was very rude because she would repeat the same phrase over and over. I expected her to say that she was doing fine and not blessed. I knew I was blessed, but I did not walk around saying it.

God had to deal with me on this issue. He had to change my perspective or view of people. I was failing to realize that the young lady was not rude, but she was really expressing who she was. She considered herself blessed. We, too, should consider ourselves as blessed. This was part of her nature and she did not compromise who she was to anyone.

Just like me, many others do not fully understand the concept of being blessed. I am quite sure that the young lady had problems and did not have the best financial status, but her attitude was such that she considered herself blessed just as the Word of God says.

We, as believers, need to learn to align our lips with the Word. We should learn to say what God says about our lives. Too often we find ourselves saying things that we should not be saying. If God says that you and I are blessed, then we are exactly what He says.

Our destiny is in our words. What we say out of our mouth is a good indication of what is going on in our heart. Jesus began to tell those wicked Pharisees in Luke 12:34 that their hearts were evil and they could not begin to speak well. Jesus further stated, "... for out of the abundance of the heart the mouth speaketh." This lets us know that the very things that we say will have a condemning effect. Therefore, we must learn to say that we are blessed even if the outside circumstances say something different. We are blessed not because we are good, but because God is good to us. Being blessed simply means being dealt with favorably by God. Although the circumstances may make it appear that you are not blessed, God says that you are. Our perception of being blessed has been tainted by the world system of material gain. The world places emphasis on fashion, cars and glamour. These external forces have a way of clouding our view of being blessed.

This is not to say that God does not bless us with material possessions. He does. He wants to bless us physically, but some of our physical blessings are not obtained because we do not heed the spiritual. We must put first things first. The spiritual must be primary in order to be blessed in the way that God would have us.

Ephesians 1:3 tells us that we have been blessed with... "all spiritual blessings in heavenly places in Christ." This means that all of our blessings are from heaven by our Lord and Savior, Jesus Christ. Although some of our blessings are physical, they have been ordained in heaven. Many times we have a tendency to separate the physical blessings from the spiritual. They should go hand in hand.

We cannot begin to thank God for our physical food and not look at it from the divine viewpoint. It was divinely planned that we would be blessed with physical blessings. God's divine blessings that are settled in heaven are made manifest to us in the physical.

Moreover, in conjunction with being blessed with all spiritual blessings, comes the view of being: chosen, accepted, predestined, redeemed, forgiven, receiving wisdom, and gaining inheritance (Ephesians 1: 4-14). These are only a few blessings that we have credited to our account. However, there are many more waiting to be claimed by the believer.

Blessed, Not Lucky

Countless times we have heard people say that you are lucky or you have lots of luck. What does this mean? What is the believer's position on luck? Many people have used the word lucky and blessed interchangeably. There is a difference. Blessed is being dealt with favorably by God, and luck is taking a chance on a matter that an event will take place, according to Webster's New World Dictionary. Being blessed implies that one is dependent upon God to bestow His glory upon you. However, luck is dependent upon the situation. Luck from a spiritual vantage point is a form of divination or witchcraft; it carries with it the weight of relying on other measures to predict that an event will or will not happen. Many of us see the spirit of divination working in the world today through psychics, gambling, witches, warlocks and even devices such as dice. Luck does not carry any godly spirituality. Instead, it carries with it a spirit of greed and lust. Luck breeds lust or covetousness. It does not involve any faith or belief in the giver of blessings.

I am so appalled when I hear a Christian say, "Knock on wood." What does knocking on wood have to do with being dealt with favorably by God? Does the wood have some quality that God does not? This phrase is one we have adopted by tradition. Moreover, since this has been learned through tradition, it is time for us to unlearn these thoughts. Luck is one word that we as believers need to take out of our vocabulary. We are not creatures of chance. We are creatures of faith.

We do not rely on any circumstance to dictate our path in life. Our compass is our faith. Faith moves us from glory to glory and from blessing to blessing. We should not be moved by what we see, but by faith (II Corinthians 5:7).

If we are going to walk in heavenly authority, we must learn to walk in faith. Faith is the very tool that is needed to walk in victory. "This is the victory that overcometh the world, even our faith" (I John 5:4b).

You cannot walk in faith believing in luck. It is not in a believer's makeup. If you are claiming to be walking by faith and speaking of luck, you are considered to be double-minded. For James 1:8 says, "A double-minded man is unstable in all his ways." You cannot make spiritual decisions because you are walking "two-headed." Two-headedness causes chaos. It causes friction and, most of all, it leads to doom.

You and I must learn to call ourselves blessed. We must speak blessings in our lives and not curses. When we speak luck into existence, we are actually speaking destruction. Believers should have the same mentality as God. Our God is a blessed God and we are blessed people. This is our position. We are blessed.

I Am Healed – I Peter 2:21-24

"For even hereunto were ye called: because Christ also suffered for us, leaving us an example, that we should follow his steps: who did not sin, neither was guile found in his mouth: Who, when he was reviled, reviled not again; when he suffered, he threatened not: but committed himself to him that judgeth righteously: Who his own self bare our sins in his own body on the tree that we, being dead to sins, should live unto righteousness, by whose stripes ye were healed."

In order to get the full scope of walking in heavenly authority, I do believe that a section on healing needs to be addressed. We cannot witness to the hurting if we do not understand healing. Healing is an attribute of our God. He is called Jehovah Rophe (The God that healeth thee). Healing has been at the seat of controversy in the Christian realm for many years. Why is it so hard for some Christians to accept healing when faith is supposed to be at the heart of each believer? Healing is a special manifestation through several vehicles from God to His people. Healing can come in several forms. It can be physical, spiritual (divine), or emotional. The above Scripture states that "With his stripes ye were healed." Because of this, what Jesus did at Calvary settled the healing question. Although this Scripture directly relates to salvation, it brings into context the other areas of healing mentioned earlier.

The word healing has a word origin from Soteria, meaning to be saved or healed. It implies that one has been delivered or been redeemed. Therefore, we can say that we are healed by the blood of Jesus Christ.

We must also realize that the ultimate healing was when we were delivered from sin. If you do not see a physical healing or any other type of healing, know that you are saved. I think that we have a tendency to overlook our receiving salvation as healing and focus more on the physical side. You were healed from the guilt and penalty of sin when you accepted Jesus as your personal Lord and Savior.

Every stripe that Jesus received from being beaten was a stripe for our healing. Every ounce of blood that was shed from His body was for our healing. For the Holy Scripture says, "without the shedding of blood there is no remission of sin" (Hebrews 9:22). This means that you and I could not be saved from our past, present, and future sins if it had not been for the stripes and the blood. This is something for us to shout about. We are healed by Jesus' action at Calvary.

Physical Healing

"And he was teaching in one of the synagogues on the Sabbath. And, behold, there was a woman which had a spirit of infirmity eighteen years, and was bowed together, and could in no wise lift up herself. And when Jesus saw her, he called her to him, and said unto her 'Woman, thou art loosed from thine infirmity. 'And he laid his hands on her: and immediately she was made straight and glorified God" (Luke 13:10-13).

This is one Bible instance that brings the very essence of physical healing to light. This woman was bowed or in modern day terms, she had a crooked spine for eighteen years and could not bring herself to a straight position. She was physically impaired. She could not do things that a normal woman could do. The Bible does not give this woman's age, or mention if she had any family or children. She is representative of any one of us.

Can you imagine being bowed eighteen years, trying to support yourself with no means of assistance? What impresses me about this woman is that she saw a need to be in church on the Sabbath Day. This woman could have heard that Jesus would be preaching at the synagogue that day and it motivated her to come. She probably had a struggle getting there. She may have had to climb several hills to get to church. Many people probably passed her by, but her desire was strong and she kept pressing.

And when Jesus saw her, he called to her. I have read this passage several times and I used to think that Jesus could have gone to her, but instead she came to him. I pondered and pondered this for several months, and I knew God had to give me a revelation about this case.

The reason Jesus wanted her to come to Him was to see her faithfulness. This is not to say that He could not have healed her from the pulpit, but He was concerned about seeing a sign of faithfulness. You must make the first step.

Faith is the main prerequisite for any healing. You say you want a physical healing, Jesus says, "Show me your Bible faith." He is not concerned about what social group we belong to, the amount of money we can pay for medical expenses, or even where we live. The only factor that Jesus requires for us to be healed is our Bible faith.

Jesus then turned to her before He even touched her and said, "Woman, thou art loosed from thine infirmity." This statement by Jesus was a word of agreement to her steadfast faith. In actuality, Jesus was saying, "You have already opened the door for your healing to take place because you took the necessary steps." She provided the portal or channel, that is, her faith.

I must stress that Jesus is a faith seeker. He delivers, heals, and sets free by our faith. He looks beyond the very fiber of our being and searches the inner man. He lurks between all the cracks and the crevices of the heart and sees our faith. This is wonderful!

Many of us do not walk in healing because of our faith level. We are constantly talking negatively about our sicknesses and do not allow our faith to be activated. We make statements like, "I will not ever get well," and "I will always be sick." These statements are very damaging to a Christian's faith. We have to learn not to walk around speaking bad health. Learn to speak good health.

After he laid hands on her, she immediately was healed. This immediate healing was because of her radical faith. She stepped out believing the one who called her out. If you and I step out on faith radically, I do believe that there will be some remarkable results.

Coming from a family that has a history of "alcoholics," I know the effects of radical faith. All my life I knew my dad had a problem with alcohol. It began to dictate his life. My dad was a deacon in the church (and very dutiful), but little did people know that he had a problem with alcohol. I would pray every day of my childhood that my dad would stop drinking. However, it got worse. Argument after argument, and drink after drink, things got progressively worse. His battle with alcohol affected the whole family.

As time passed, His health began to suffer and the doctor told him that he had to stop drinking or he would die. He did not listen and continued to drink. I would go from room to room, laying hands on him and everything he touched, believing that God would heal him. I remember standing at the ironing board, tears in my eyes, saying, "I need you to be my dad again." I was hurting physically as well as spiritually. I needed God to heal the situation. I was supplying the faith, and waiting on God to honor it. Within a span of a year, God stepped in and healed him and he rededicated his life to Christ. Physical healing is not impossible for God when the proper faith is supplied.

Moreover, there are times when the proper faith is supplied and there is no physical healing and we wonder what is happening. This does not mean that God is not listening or not responding. He is building character.

Sometimes God has a waiting room for His children. He allows us to sit and dwell on Him and get renewed inwardly before any deliverance takes place. This is not to say that God is not healing us or we are not supplying the proper faith; it says that we are getting pruned for our healing.

In viewing the subject of healing, we cannot overlook the area of modem medicine. God does heal through the use of modern medicine. There are some individuals who think that God does not heal through this device. You do not have to be a spiritual giant to know that God has increased the knowledge of man to create numerous types of pills or liquids that will eliminate problems. Many diseases such as polio, tuberculosis, and even some sexually transmitted diseases have been cured through the use of modern medicine. God desires for his people to walk in divine health and it is not impossible. You can be healed physically.

Spiritual Healing

"Why art thou cast down, 0 my soul? And why art thou disquieted within me? Hope thou in God: For I shall yet praise him, who is the health of my countenance, and my God." Psalm 42:11

All believers should have experienced being spiritually low at some point in their lives. This is not to say that we are not strong in our faith, but there remains a side of us that becomes downtrodden or spiritually weak.

The psalmist feels this same anguish. He introduces this Psalm with a longing to be in the presence of God. He compares himself to a deer that longs for water at the brook after a tiresome day.

In other words, the psalmist is saying that he needed to be restored. He needed to be spiritually healed. This should be the attitude of each believer. The hustle and bustle of each day, the daily struggles with the flesh and the constant warring with the devil can cause us to become spiritually weak.

As sure as there is physical healing, there is also spiritual healing. It should be mentioned that healing should be centered around the spiritual. If we learn to align our spirit man with the Word of God, that is, doing according to what it says, I do believe that our physical problems can be controlled.

When I speak of spiritual healing, I am speaking of healing that pertains to the Word of God. There may be a practice with which one is involved, which does not have any Bible implications. This is a very important point for us to remember as believers. We have to be careful or on guard for those practices that people say are spiritual, If they are not monitored, they can put you and me in spiritual jeopardy.

In order for spiritual healing to take place in the biblical sense of the word, we must deal with the circumstance just as the psalmist did. First, he recognized the problem. In Psalms 42:9-10, he says, "I will say unto God, my rock. Why hast thou forgotten me? Why go I mourning because of the oppression of the enemy? As with a sword in my bones, mine enemies reproach me; while they say daily unto me, Where is thy God?" He knew there was a part of him that controlled his emotions, his ability to serve God, and even his ability to experience peace with himself. This was affected by some external forces. He referred to his enemies as a cause of his soul being disquieted.

This is a key point for us to remember. We must recognize the cause of being spiritually low… Ask God to show you where the low point is in your life so that you can deal with it. I know I find myself being low in spirit and I try to figure out why. Most of the time, it is because I have not studied, prayed, or even meditated on the Word of God as I should.

When you are in love with someone and have not seen or talked to them in a while, it makes you feel low in spirit, You become thirsty for their affection. This is how it is with our relationship with God, You cannot miss a day thinking about Him or meditating on His acts. If it is missed, your day is not complete and a void can creep into your emotions. This makes the old cliché, "There is no place like home" a true statement. Our spiritual healing is solely dependent upon our relationship with God.

Second, the psalmist realized where his hope came from (Psalms 42:11). After we recognize where the problem lies, it should compel us to return to the one who can solve it. The psalmist also knew that he was nothing without the Lord. Everything that he was and intended to be was centered around God. That is why he says, "hope thou in God…" He was relying on God to perform his healing. He knew God was the only one that could restore his soul to its rightful place of peace.

Saints, there is a part of us that no one can heal but God. No matter how much medicine we take, or how much emotional stress training that we experience, God is our healer.

Learn to trust God for that spiritual healing you have desired. Never let anyone tell you that it cannot be done. It can.

After the psalmist realized where his hope came from, he was overwhelmed with emotion and began to release his praise to God. He says, in Psalms 42:11, "for I shall yet praise him, who is the health of my countenance and my God."

Do not forget to offer God praise for all your healings. He allowed it to be so. That is the reason the psalmist released his expression of thanksgiving to God by praising Him for his healing.

I am reminded of how Jesus healed Peter's mother-in-law from a fever and, in turn, she immediately began to offer her thanks by serving Jesus and his disciples (Luke 4:38-39). She realized that she should give thanks to those who ministered to her. This is the attitude that we should all adopt. When God performs a spiritual healing or any type of healing, we should learn to serve God by giving Him praise for His marvelous acts.

However, there are those who let their thanks to God go unspoken. We can get so elated about our spiritual healing and forget to render the proper honor to God. This was the case with the nine lepers that were healed by Jesus. Only one came back to render praise for his healing.

Finally, the psalmist also says in Psalms 42:11, that, "God is the health of my countenance, and my God." This implies that God is the antidote for his spiritual healing. Notice, he did not say God was, but is. Although this psalm was written during Old Testament times, it still has present day application. The Lord is still the health of our countenance. No matter what has caused your spiritual health to decline, I say to you with authority—there is healing for you today and His name is Jesus.

Chapter 10
Get Up and Accept Your Authority

Joshua 1:2-3

Arise, stand up, gird yourself, it is now time for you to take your proper position! Your season has arrived. The flowers are blooming. The fruit is ready to be picked. Your time is now.

After we have gained a thorough understanding of who we are and have been trained in our field of knowledge, it should inspire us believers to rise and lay claim to the position in which we have been called. When we have been called, groomed, and equipped to perform a specific task, there should be a measure of zeal that we possess. We should not house a lazy, unwilling spirit. We should always be open to the dictates of God's will.

After Moses died, God knew that His work must go on. He had promised Abraham that his descendants would be blessed and that they would be brought into that land He had promised (Genesis 17:6-8). God made a vow to Abraham and that vow was passed down from generation to generation. Moses' death did not hinder or discount the promises that God made to Abraham. God always has a way to carry His plan through to completion. Moses' death yielded a stepping-stone for his minister, Joshua. After several years of watching the leadership, hearing the teaching, and viewing the techniques of Moses, Joshua was now ready to assume the leadership of the nation of Israel. It was now his time to rise and take hold of the baton.

Many of you might be saying, 'this was a commission for Joshua to perform a specific task, but this does not pertain to me. If we would really take into account the prior chapters on authority and the duty that we have, it should invoke a spirit of zeal in each of us.

Just because some of us are not in positions that offer fancy titles that declare authority, does not mean that you are not in authority. When you and I were chosen to be in the family of God and accepted the call, we were obligated to be in authority. Jesus also told us to occupy until He returns (Luke 19:13). Although this message from Jesus is spoken in parabolic language, it does not water down the message that is given to us as believers. That is, the position of leadership and authority does not lie in the hands of the world, but in the hearts and hands of His saints.

We cannot say that we are saints of God in the truest fashion and can never lay human claim to the authority that has been laid for us. Authority cannot be claimed unless someone claims it. It must have a host to make use of it. You are that host.

After Moses died, God could have singled out anyone besides Joshua to carry on the work, but Joshua was next in line. He fit the criteria. So it is with each and every believer. We have been fitted to carry the baton that Jesus left. When He left physically from the earth, the authority was passed down to those who were next in line. We are the carriers of the Good News of Jesus Christ. Jesus has no hands but our hands. We are the vessels that are fit to take charge of the duties at hand. So rise, stand, and take your appointed place.

No Fear

"Have not I commanded thee? Be strong and of a good courage; be not afraid, neither be thou dismayed: for the Lord thy God is with thee whithersoever thou goest. Joshua 1:9

Whenever any child of God is called upon to take a position for Christ, there should not be any fear. Fear is not an attribute of God. And it should not be a part of the nature of the believer.

Notice, I said there should not be. After one receives information that goes against what is normal, conversation can cause some nerves to rise. But after one receives it, then faith should take its proper place. Everything that we hear or do should be centered around faith. Many times we can psych ourselves up to be super-human and say that we do not have sudden fears or nervousness. It is possible that these sudden panic attacks occur because we are not always in the spiritual realm. Fear has a way of trying to steal our faith. It causes our peace to be unsettled. It causes unrest and God always reminds us that "our unrest is the devil's fuel." Unrest is the devil's way of trying to take the saints out of their proper authority. He knows that if he can get our whole being to fear, then that places a thorn in our side to prevent us from carrying out God's plans.

From Joshua 1:9, God had commanded Joshua to stand and take his authority. God knew the human side of Joshua, as He does with us. He knew that Joshua would be sort of fearful at the onset, and he would need to be encouraged.

Therefore, He tells him to "Be strong, and of a good courage." For a long time I wondered why God told Joshua to be of "a good courage," when courage is looked upon as being good. The Holy Spirit and a dear friend revealed to me that all courage is not good. It has to be motivated by the right force. God, in essence, is saying, "Do not get caught up in being Joshua and in all the battles you have fought." Instead, God is saying, trust Me.

When God calls us for a task, we have a tendency to get caught up in our past accomplishments and how we have triumphed. And throughout all the self-promotion, we leave the main contributor out of the picture. Deuteronomy 8:17 warns us not to say that we have become prosperous on our own. We must learn to keep first things first because there is a danger when we forget God. Moreover, God never calls us without encouraging us. He told Joshua not to be afraid nor dismayed because God's everlasting presence was with him. Although sudden fear prompts the heart to plunge deeper into fear, God calls out encouragement to pull us out of fear.

I am reminded that there are times when God has spoken a command that is only fit for you and, once it is made known, the devil uses certain people to try to invoke fear. He will try and use them to talk you out of the vision that God has given you.

There are times when God tells me something he wants me to do and I want to immediately run and tell someone else, but I have to remember that everyone will not celebrate with my heavenly vision. Instead, they will try and talk me out of it. So therefore, I have learned to be quiet until God tells me to speak. This may sound kind of backwoodish, but I do believe in its wisdom.

Finally, when I speak of "No Fear," I am not saying that we should not fear. There should only be one type of fear that we possess and that is reverential fear. This lets us know that all fear is not bad. God has called us to fear Him. Psalm 34:9 says, "O fear the Lord, ye his saints: for there is no want to them that fear him." Reverential fear is a part of our duty to God. He commands us to fear, that is, to respect Him. When we disrespect His commands, it shows a lack of fear for God.

Joshua could have dismissed the commands of God and displayed a lack of reverential fear. If you notice in Joshua 1:10-11, Joshua Moreover, God never calls us without encouraging us. He told Joshua not to be afraid nor dismayed because God's everlasting presence was with him. Although sudden fear prompts the heart to plunge deeper into fear, God calls out encouragement to pull us out of fear.

This is a beautiful passage of reverential fear. The passage says in verses 10-11, "Then Joshua commanded the officers of the people, saying, 'Pass through the host, and command the people, saying, prepare you victuals; for within three days ye shall pass over this Jordan, to go in to possess the land, which the Lord your God giveth you to possess it.'"

Joshua knew the promise God had spoken to him and that God would be with him. As a result of this command being spoken to Joshua, he humbled himself and submitted to what God had called him to perform.

This is a lesson in itself. When we come under the authority of another, we must learn to show reverence for the person by submitting ourselves. Too often we want to be in authority, but we forget about the air of submission that goes along with the position.

A proverb that God has put into my spirit is that "before we can learn to walk in heavenly authority, we must learn the power of submission." When we submit ourselves to God and His purpose, then our authority can begin to manifest itself in a more excellent way.

SECTION THREE

Utilizing Your Authority

CHAPTER 11
Using Your Authority Over Intimidation

"And in nothing terrified by your adversaries: which is to them an evident token of perdition, but to you of salvation, and that of God. For unto you it is given in the behalf of Christ, not only to believe on him, but also to suffer for his sake; Having the same conflict which ye saw in me, and now hear to be in me." (Philippians 1:28-30).

Have you ever felt threatened by a situation or a person? Did the situation make you feel as if you were the lowest person around? Did it affect your ability to cope with that situation? Were you afraid to come into the presence of that person? These questions and several others are characteristic of intimidation.

Intimidation is a word that we often use, but we rarely talk about how to counteract it. So many times we become so saturated with who is doing the intimidating, and forget about the one who is really behind the ploy.

The word intimidation takes it origin from one not being confident in himself or who his God is. This may sound rather foreign to some of us, but it is truth. When one is fully aware of who they really are, then intimidation will not manifest itself. You must know your position in the kingdom of God, otherwise, the devil will us all types of deceit to manipulate you.

Intimidation also means that one's character and personality have been reduced to fear, panic attacks, and having no self-confidence. This is a tool the devil uses to belittle the people of God.

The main Scripture reference, Philippians 1:28, from the Amplified Bible states, "And do not [for a moment] be frightened or intimidated in anything by your opponents and adversaries, for such [constancy and fearlessness] will be a clear sign (proof and seal) to them of [their impending] destruction, but [a sure token and evidence] of your deliverance and salvation, and that from God."

This Scripture declares to you and me that we should not be moved by momentary fear or any type of intimidation. Fear breeds instability. Intimidation causes us to be off balance and places us in a position of being out of control. It also causes our whole realm of peace to be disturbed, which, in turn, will move us out of operating the way God would have us to.

Realistically speaking, some of you may be saying, 'how am I supposed to act when the spirit of intimidation comes against me?' Do I just stand there and let the enemy overtake me? No, I am not expressing this view, but what I am declaring to you is that you must not give way to the spirit of intimidation. Do not let it overwhelm you. And most of all, do not allow it to move you out of what God has called you into. I know from a natural point of view that it seems close to impossible, but this is not natural. It is supernatural. And the way that you handle a supernatural spirit is by using a supernatural force. Our supernatural force is the Holy Ghost.

This is so important for us to realize. Moreover, we must not fight a supernatural force with a physical force. It cannot be won by those means. This is the reason Apostle Paul addresses the Corinthian Church in his second letter, stating "For the weapons of our warfare are not carnal [worldly, fleshly], but mighty through God to the pulling down of strongholds" (2 Corinthians 10:4).

I remember when I was in a pressing job situation and the devil was using the bosses in a crafty way. They tried to throw their weight or seniority around to belittle me. It made me so upset. Some days I would just go into the restroom or go home and cry. I did not know how to handle this intimidation. God had to train me in this area. He began to tell me to stand still and not to be moved by what I saw or heard. I did not know that this was a weapon against the enemy. As a result of my not seeking revenge against my enemies, the spirit of intimidation had to fall back into the pit of hell. I had to let the devil know that I was in control by the authority of Jesus Christ. This is what we have to say to this situation. We do not have to always say it to the person being used by the devil, but we should learn to speak it out of our mouths so the devil can hear it. After all, he does have big ears. Philippians 1:28 declares that when we do not allow this spirit to overwhelm us, this will be a sign to the enemy that he has been defeated and will also be a sign of the believer's overwhelming deliverance. We have already been delivered from this spirit of intimidation, but we do not understand how to unlock the necessary tools that have been already instilled.

Moreover, in the Scriptural text, Apostle Paul knew that the enemy had placed some Judases into the path of this church. He was preparing them to be on guard against this type of spirit. This spirit did not only run rampant in biblical times, but it is manifesting its presence in a bold way today.

How do we handle this? What other techniques are available to the believer? How can we put them into action? Hopefully, this next section will teach us how we can better deal with this spirit.

Three Steps to Overcoming Intimidation

"Ye are of God, little children, and have overcome them: because greater is he that is in you than he that is in the world" (I John 4:4).

While I was going through one of the most traumatic times in my life, God revealed this Scripture in a mighty way to me. I also use this Scripture when I am teaching the youth at my church (they can probably quote it in their sleep and may even be tired of it). Nevertheless, it teaches us the importance of who we are. This is how we learn to cope and use the authority that we have because we are now made aware of who we are.

Below are three necessary steps that will aid in dealing with intimidation:

Know your position in God (I John 4:4a). John is instructing believers that in order to overcome the devil and all of his devices, you must know your position. Too often we run from the oppressor instead of running toward him because we are unaware of our position. This verse also informs us of where we originated spiritually. The Scripture states, "Ye are of God, little children." We were created and empowered by the one who has all power. We are the descendants of the Man of war and the One who is mighty in battle. Knowing this, we can now be positioned in such a way that intimidation can no longer rob us of the authority that we have been given. Remember, we are the trees of righteousness and the planting of the Lord (Isaiah 61:3). That is, we have been rooted in the Main Root, our Lord and Savior, Jesus Christ.

Know your present victory in God (vs. 4b). This part of the Scripture is so mind-boggling. It already assesses our status of overcoming any situation. It tells us that we "have overcome them [the devil and his demonic forces]." This is assuredly why you and I should not allow ourselves to wallow in self-pity and self-denial because God through Jesus Christ completed the whole mission concerning the destiny of the devil and his spirits. The devil has already been committed to hell. When this factor is acknowledged, we can begin to rebuild our self-confidence and morale. The only thing that we need to do now is rest and stand on our present victory.

Know your power in God (vs. 4e). This part of the Scripture has come to be one of the most quoted in our churches, but how well are we letting it override our problems? The Scripture says, "... because greater is he that is in you, than he that is in the world." When I view this verse, I see that there are two powers. Both have power, but God indwelling the believer is greater. What does this say about intimidation? If this spirit is trying to take control of you, rely on the greater power you have on the inside to overtake it. Church, God is greater than any situation. If we allow the "Great I Am" on the inside of us to rule, then this fight with intimidation will only serve as a testimony of the delivering power of the Authoritative One. Learn how to use your power.

The Goliath Intimidation Factor

"And he stood and cried unto the armies of Israel, and said unto them, 'Why are ye come out to set your battle in array? Am not I a Philistine, and ye servants to Saul? Choose you a man for you and let him come down to me. If he be able to fight with me and to kill me, then will we be your servants: but if I prevail against him and kill him, then shall ye be our servants, and serve us'---When Saul and all Israel heard those words of the Philistine, they were dismayed, and greatly afraid." I Samuel 17:8-9, 11

Out of all the times that I have read this story, I have never looked at it as an "intimidation factor." What makes this scene an intimidation factor is that one is constantly reminded of one's ability or strong suit. In the case of Goliath, it was his intimidating height, background, and strength.

Goliath was so adamant and prideful of his outer extremities and was always looking down on others. Is this not just like the devil? Goliath in this passage could be considered a type of Lucifer. He uses his might and background as tools to intimidate the children of Israel.

As mentioned earlier, with intimidation comes a bit of pride. Goliath knew that the Philistines were a military that had the greatest of war materials. He also knew that if he could use these factors to try to belittle the children of Israel, this would put a measure of fear in them and they would lose focus. This is exactly how the enemy operates. He will use any factor that would be advantageous to him to degrade others.

Goliath even went as far as to make a bargain with the children of Israel just as the devil did with Jesus in the wilderness (Matthew 4:1-11). Goliath knew that there was no way possible that any of them could beat him in the natural. This was only a trap by Goliath and little did he know that he was also setting up his own destiny.

What I really want to convey throughout this section is how intimidation is not a new tactic or a new action, but that it has been in existence since biblical times. With this thought in mind, we see in this Scriptural text how the devil was at work. Through the strong will of Goliath and the intimidation of the King, the children of Israel were forced into a saddening position.

First Samuel 17:11 states, "When Saul and all Israel heard those words of the Philistine, they were dismayed, and greatly afraid." This is very sad because they did not realize the effect Goliath's words had on them. It forced them out of control and delegated the authority that was theirs to Goliath. Goliath's words fostered fear in God's people. Those words created an atmosphere of utter panic. We can only imagine what was going on in the minds of God's people. Some could have had panic attacks every time they heard the name Goliath. Some could have rendered themselves as hopeless beings.

Do not allow what people say to cause you to be in disarray. Remember what God says about you in His Word. I came to this realization in my life. It does not matter what others think or say about you, but it does matter what God thinks about you. Now, whose report are you going to believe—the lies of the devil or the truth of God?

This view of the Goliath intimidation factor is all too common. I remember the state that the devil left me in. I appeared to be hopeless, having no life. I felt drained, depressed, and even thought about giving up. These Goliath factors caused me to be in a state of unrest and insecurity.

Some of you may be experiencing a few of the same factors that I encountered. I admonish you today not to give up or give in. I am a living witness that God will always raise up a standard when the enemy comes in like a flood (Isaiah 59:19).

The Reflection of David

"And David said to Saul, 'Let no man's heart fail because of him; thy servant will go and fight with this Philistine'... David said moreover, The Lord that delivered me out of the paw of the lion, and out of the paw of the bear, he will deliver me out of the hand of this Philistine.' And Saul said unto David, "Go, and the Lord be with thee" (I Samuel 17:32, 37).

As a result of the intimidation of Goliath, the whole camp was in total uproar. When David came back from tending to his father's sheep, he asked what needed to be done to take out this Philistine. David was confident that he could beat Goliath and his confident words were taken before King Saul.

David was not being arrogant about the matter, but he was being confident. He was speaking from experience. He was also speaking prophetically. He knew within his heart that he could defeat Goliath. Although other Israelites were intimidated, David was not. He stood firm on his convictions.

What made David so sure? What made him think that he could defeat this larger-than-life man? What made David not to be moved by the intimidation of Goliath? David relied upon his reflections. He knew the power of reflecting. He knew somewhere in the back of his memories were the very keys to overcoming Goliath. Goliath stood before David as a reminder of the past trials that he had endured. David also remembered how the Lord allowed him to defeat the lion and bear. He knew that if he would face the present situation by viewing how he overcame the past, it would give him the key to his victory.

This is a lesson for all of God's children. God is teaching us something through the character of a young lad. He wants us to use the power of reflection to serve as a reminder that we can overcome the present. Reflections of how God delivered us out of a past situation should remind us of how He will deliver us out of our current situations.

With this reflection comes a weight of authority. David could now transfer what he had learned from the reflection into positional weight. He could now speak with authority of his ability to overthrow any foe that came into his presence. I say to you, dear saints, use your past experiences with God as authoritative weight. You do not have to be arrogant about it, but you can speak with confidence that God is able to deliver you out of any attack of the enemy.

I really like what David said in I Samuel 17:32. "And David said to Saul, Let no man's heart fail because of him ...." If you will allow me to personalize this statement like this, "Do not worry, lose sleep, or have heart trouble over this man, Goliath, I will take care of him." In this Scriptural reference, David represents that side of us that is operating in faith. He was not walking by what the circumstances indicated, nor by what Goliath looked like, but he was walking by the counsel of God.

This is the hour in which faith needs to be the key to overcoming intimidation. Although our personal Goliaths seem to be so pressing, tiring, troublesome, and even intimidating, we need to learn how to invoke faith. If you are going to possess the strength and the spirit of David, you must learn how to walk in light of faith. Learn to be a faith warrior. The Bible says, "For whatsoever is born of God overcometh the world: and this is victory that overcometh the world, even our faith" (I John 5:4). You can overcome intimidation.

Chapter 12
Using the Authority of the Blood

"And the blood shall be to you for a token upon the houses where ye are: and when I see the blood, I will pass over you, and the plague shall not be upon you to destroy you, when I smite the land of Egypt."-Exodus 12:13

Have you ever really thought about the great weight that blood carries? It contains certain DNA and tissues that allow the body to be formed into the specimen that it is. Blood from a human standpoint reveals one's eye color, genetic structure, hair texture, body and frame makeup, and aids in determining gender.

In history, man has taken blood and extracted it to create clones of animals. We have seen test tube babies, blood transfusions, and even successful usages in donating blood. Blood, in essence, is one of the building blocks of society. It is what God designed from the beginning of time to craft us and create us as unique individuals.

Given these uses of blood, they allow us to see the dramatic comparison of why blood was so important from a spiritual standpoint.

"What can wash away my sin? Nothing but the Blood of Jesus. What can make me whole again? Nothing but the Blood of Jesus. Oh precious is the flow that makes me white as snow, no other fount I know, nothing but the Blood of Jesus" (Robert Lory).

Robert Lory was correct in saying the blood (of Jesus) was the only element that could make us clean. Blood, in general, leaves a stain, but the blood of Christ cleans stains. Moreover, the blood of Jesus Christ served and still serves as a cleansing agent against the sin that had infected us through our fore-parents, Adam and Eve. Since we were separated from God, the authority of the blood was the only tool that could bring us back into right standing with our Heavenly Father. For the Bible says, "...and without the shedding of blood is no remission [of sin]" (Hebrews 9:22).

Exodus 12:13 brings to light the history of how we are now able to use the Blood of Christ in our present-day situation. During the period of Israelite captivity in Egypt, God sent Moses to inform Pharaoh to let His people go. Several signs and wonders were performed to persuade Pharaoh of the urgency of the matter. One of the plagues used by God to cast judgment on Israel was to allow a spirit of death to cover the land. This spirit would cause all the male babies to be put to death whose houses were not covered with the blood of an unblemished lamb. And for those whose houses were covered with the blood, the death spirit would pass over the house. However, this blood covering is symbolic of Jesus Christ being our Passover Lamb (I Corinthians 5:7).

Exodus 12:13 states, "And the blood shall be to you a token upon the houses where ye are: and when I see the blood and pass over you, the plague shall not be upon you to destroy you when I smite the land of Egypt." This lets us know that blood serves as a covering for God's people. Although this Scripture speaks specifically of a covering for the first male child during this time, it also sends a great message to us.

Since Jesus has redeemed us by the shedding of His blood, we have also been covered. This blood does not only cover our sins, but it also covers everything that concerns us.

"The blood shall be to you a token upon the houses where ye are…" From a spiritual standpoint, the Body of Christ is a spiritual house made up of many individuals, but all individuals have the same blood covering. First Peter 1:18-19 declares, that we have not been redeemed by corruptible things such as silver and gold…. but with the precious blood of Christ." Peter used a strong adjective to describe the significance of the Blood of Christ. He stated that it was "precious." When an item is precious, it is a rare commodity, and a very high cost would be paid for the item. So it is with Christ's blood. It is precious. Therefore, we have been purchased with high value.

When the Scripture states that the blood is a token, this serves as symbolism to you and me that it represents authority. Although it is a token, it is not subject to being taken from us. The blood of Jesus was given as a constant reminder that He is always cleansing us. Whenever we approach the throne of grace, Jesus is not only looking at faith, but He is looking for the token of blood. This is one reason why everyone cannot approach God in prayer. All people have not been covered by the blood of Jesus.

The Blood of Jesus Clears All Deadness

"For if the blood of bulls and of goats, and the ashes of an heifer sprinkling the unclean, sanctifieth to the purifying of the flesh: How much more shall the blood of Christ, who through the eternal Spirit offered himself without spot to God, purge your conscience from dead works to serve the living God?" Hebrews 9:13-14

This Scripture is so special in that it places a comparison of the Old Testament and the New Testament. The shed blood of bulls, goats, and heifers represents the cutting away of deadness by the Old Testament and the Blood of Jesus represents the clearing away of all sin (deadness) declared in the New Testament. What is the difference? The difference is that Christ has obtained a more excellent ministry, "… (He) is the mediator of a better covenant, which was established upon better promises (Hebrews 8:6)." Although the covenant of using the blood of goats and heifers served its time, it could not satisfy the sin debt that we acquired. This ceremony required a constant sacrifice of animals to atone for sin. However, it took a holy lamb that could identify with our spiritual nature and also our humanity to clean us forever.

Not only was the blood covenant of Jesus Christ founded on better principles, it is also able to clean our conscience (Hebrews 9:14). This is the part of humanity that really needs to be cleaned. With all of the deceptive thoughts inspired by the devil, all the manipulative plans that we have planted in our minds—we need our minds cleaned. Romans 12:2 tell us to be transformed by the renewing of our minds. If the animal's blood was able to clean up situations, the blood of Jesus cleans much more.

Now it is time for us as believers to break away from things that hinder our growth. There are some things that we are attached to that need to be cut off. There may be someone who has an alcoholic problem, drug addiction, or a struggle with depression or suicide. It is now time to allow the authority of the blood to take root in your life. So many believers are tied down to things that they are greater than and are unaware of it. I am reminded of the scenario in Exodus 1:9 where the Israelites were in bondage and a new king was on the throne. He said, "Behold, the people of the children of Israel are more and mightier than we." All the king was saying was that Israel was entangled in a system that could not contain them. The king knew the power the Israelites had, but the sad thing is that the Israelites did not. It is a sad feeling to watch a decline of a people when we know that there is a remedy.

There may be a dead family situation that someone may be holding on to, but it is time we use the token (the authority of Jesus' blood) that was left to us. The blood of Jesus allows dead situations to be resurrected. He did it for us. Your dead situation may be a consuming job, a disobedient child, or even a dead church congregation. Whatever the case may be, the Blood of Jesus can clean it up.

Chapter 13

Using the Word of Your Testimony

"And they overcame him by the blood of the Lamb, and by the word of their testimony." Revelation 12:11

Throughout my fellowshipping with my home church, I have been taught the power of words. Rev. Clyde Beverly, Sr. would always whisper, "You can never underestimate the power of words, for wars have been fought over words." This statement has stuck with me throughout my Christian life. I never knew the impact that words could have on any situation until he spoke them to me.

Words display our emotions, our intellect, and our ability to communicate. They also serve as a vehicle to heal wounds, give comfort, and cause death. They invite us to share with others who speak languages that are not our own. Moreover, words are the means in which God used to create the world. Without words, we can never know the impact that we can make until the words are spoken.

Given this information on words, have you ever thought about the word of your testimony? Your testimony has the power to speak life into a dead situation. When you use your testimony as a witnessing tool to attest to the delivering power of God, you are using the word of your testimony. You are standing assured that God is able to deliver you.

Revelation 12:11, states, "And they overcame him by the blood of the Lamb and by the word of their testimony." It should be mentioned that we cannot separate the blood of the Lamb from witnessing what the blood of the Lamb did. The blood of the Lamb, as mentioned in the previous chapter, is the main ingredient for salvation. If Jesus had not died and shed blood, we could not have a true testimony. For a testimony is based upon a person being tested, and the end result yields a positive or negative report. Prophetically speaking, this Scripture views the church as being in a contest or in contention with the devil and it also declares the outcome of the contest: the church is victorious. How does this Scripture relate in utilizing one's authority? It declares to you and me the mode by which authority is released. The Scripture says, "by the Word." This is one of the channels by which the believer operates, survives, and continues to gain victory.

Speak the Word

"…The word is nigh thee, even in thy mouth, and in thy heart: that is, the word of faith which we preach" Romans 10:8.

"…for out of the abundance of the heart the mouth speaketh" Matthew12:34.

We are the possessors of destiny. The authority of speaking destiny is in our mouths. We have the power to bring into existence any good or bad thing in our lives by the words we speak. Sometimes we are unaware of the things that we speak into our lives, thereby leaving us in places that we should not dwell.

When I speak of "speaking the Word," I am talking in respect to declaring the truth of God's Word. Moreover, this can also be looked upon as confessing the Word of God with confidence. When we speak God's Word with confidence, we are relying totally on the power of the Word to do a work for us. We are assured that God is able to perform His Word that was spoken out of our mouths. This type of speaking is an authoritative method that all Christians should learn to do.

The aforementioned Scriptures declare that the Word of God is in our mouths and also in our hearts. These are the portals by which the Word is carried and spoken. For the Scripture also says that out of the abundance of the heart the mouth speaks. What is planted in your heart? What type of thoughts are you harboring in your heart? Are they good thoughts? Do they edify God and the body of Christ? These are very important questions for us to ponder because they allow us to do a soul search into our innermost being and detect if we are sincere or not.

As stated earlier, you have the power to change your whole atmosphere or destiny by what you think and say. I remember a young lady in our church who had been diagnosed with multiple sclerosis.

She came to church one Sunday and the Spirit led her to get up and speak and give her testimony after missing the first Sunday's service of the new year. She got up and began to say, "I do not know if you all can understand me because my speech is so slurred. However, I want you to know that the devil did not want me to speak or give my testimony, but he is a liar. I said to him that I will give my testimony because God is so good to me even in my affliction."

And after she finished giving her testimony, the power of God began to move in the church congregation. People were released from the bondages that held them, testimonies went boldly forth, and a soul was added to the kingdom. Furthermore, the preacher could not speak or give a message because the power of God was thick in the sanctuary.

This young lady's testimony was the catalyst for invoking the power of God to move. By the use of her testimony, the devil was defeated and glory was given to God (Revelation 12:11). I declare that if you begin to confess the Word of God boldly, your atmosphere will change. I have come to realize that God does not care how bad our situations may be, but when one "speaks the Word," they are opening the door for God to move. This is the reason why Paul could say to the church at Rome, that "The word is nigh thee, even in thy mouth, and in thy heart: that is, the word of faith which we preach." Paul knew that when the Word of God was close to anyone, things were subject to change. For the resulting change is based upon one's confession (Romans 10:9).

Confession is primarily saying what God has said about a situation. This is a key point throughout this whole chapter. If we learn to call things the way God calls them, then we are operating in the safety zone and out of delegated authority. We must learn from the example of God when He begins to call things which are not as though they were and as they came to be (Romans 4:17). I am mighty afraid that many Christians are walking around living defeated lives because of failing to speak God's Word over their circumstances. Even if the situation does not get better immediately, continue to say, I believe what God says: "I am the righteousness of God, no weapon formed against me shall prosper, and nothing can separate me from the love of God. I am a new creature; old things are passed away and behold all things are made new." This kind of thinking goes against the carnal thinking pattern. Remember, you are not operating by the standards that the world operates. You are under a different covering that operates under different principles and morals.

Many people will laugh at you because you are saying what God says in His Word. You will be ridiculed because of the things of the Spirit, but be encouraged that the words that you begin to speak are declarations to the fact that you are walking in the authority of God and walking according to His principles.

Be a Radical Abraham

"Who against hope believed in hope, that he might become the father of many nations; according to that which was spoken, So shall thy seed be. And being not weak in faith, he considered not his own body now dead, when he was about an hundred years old, neither yet the deadness of Sarah's womb. He staggered not at the promises of God through unbelief; but was strong in faith, giving glory to God; And being fully persuaded that, what he had promised, he was able also to perform. "Romans 4:18-21

What testimony did Abraham have? Abraham was bound by the testimony of faith. It was founded on the promise that God had made to him and his seed. It is so good to know that God backs His Word by His Word. He does not need anyone to vouch for Him. His word is righteous and His testimonies are sure (final, confident, sealed, concrete, set in stone).

What was so different about Abraham? He was a man like you and me. He had problems like you and me. Overall, he was human like you and me. But what made him so different? He had a quality that is unlike the norm, that is, he was radical in His faith. He took the testimony of God and became radical in his believing God. The word radical means that one goes to the extreme or goes beyond the norm. All Bible faith should be radical. Many times we just say with the mouth that we have faith, but faith becomes radical when we put some corresponding action behind it. Nevertheless, Abraham began to speak like God wanted him to. God unveiled four things to me that made Abraham radical in faith:

He hoped when it seemed as if there was no hope (Romans 8:8). It would seem logical that when a person sees that there is no hope, they would "throw in the towel." He did not allow the "give-up spirit" to override the promise that God had made to him. He was standing in expectation for God to move in the fashion that He had promised. Abraham knew that if he would just wait, the promise would come to full effect. Moreover, there is a deeper anointing that we can have when we wait and expect God to move. Our enthusiasm becomes greater, our zeal becomes more exciting, our worries are less, and finally our faith is strengthened. Expectation or hoping is one of the main keys that is needed on the part of a believer when walking in heavenly authority. This causes us to be more effective because of the optimism that is present in our lives. You have got to expect the best to happen before it comes into fruition.

"He considered not his own body now dead "(Romans 4:19). I am assured that being considerate of something God says is crucial. Not to consider is one of the tools that hinders a believer's authority. As stated in previous chapters, you have to know who you are in Christ. Many times believers consider themselves or their circumstances dead based upon what someone else has expressed to them. I am declaring to you today that you must believe the report of God. If He told you that you are going to be blessed, then that is what you have to consider yourself. Learn to consider what God considers true. I have learned to speak out of my mouth the promises that God has spoken to me from His Word. When I am feeling like I have not done right, I begin to quote that "I am the righteousness of God."

When I am going through the floods of life, I begin to speak the words, "When thou passeth through the waters I am with thee." This is reaffirmation of what God tells us from His Word, This is the same principle that Abraham had to express to himself. He had to consider his body alive. If he had viewed his body from the natural perspective, depression could have easily set in. But he decided to see his body as alive and functioning. Remember, you are what you consider yourself.

Abraham did not stagger at the promise through unbelief, but was strong in faith (Romans 4:20). Have you ever taken the time to think about what staggering really is? Many times we are prone to think of a drunken man who wobbles as he walks to his destination. This is exactly what staggering is when put into action. The Greek translation views staggering in the position of wavering or doubting. Staggering from the spiritual standpoint is caused by a believer being negatively influenced by an internal or external force. The outside or external force may be a family member that tries to talk you out of the promise that God has made to you. It may be the enticement of a desire that tries to trick you out of the promise. Nevertheless, we are assured that these outside or external forces can hinder us from claiming the promise of God. Staggering is a dangerous position to be in. It releases one's ability to walk effectively in authority. It also causes us to be wishy-washy. When we waver in our faith, we become unstable. We cannot truly operate the way God would have us do because of our instability. We need most of all, in times such as these to become focused on God. When this is done, it places us back on target. It revives us to the rightful place that God would have us to be. Abraham, however, knew that if he would stagger like a drunken man, his faith would waver, the promise would be left unclaimed and, most importantly, his seed could not be the recipients of the blessing. This is something for us to think about.

He was fully persuaded concerning the promise (Romans 4:21). Abraham was self-assured and God-assured that the promise would come to pass. He did not have an inkling of a doubt that God might not do according to what He promised. The word 'fully' in this text changes the tone of the message. It allows us to view the mind of Abraham at this time. This word fully means that he was thoroughly convinced, no reservations, no hidden questions or insecurity concerning the will of God. Often, many of us are torn emotionally when things do not happen in a timely fashion. In essence, we think that the quiet times in our lives are signs that God is not working on our behalf. With this in mind, have you ever considered that God is allowing time to foster patience in you that was not there during those silent years?

I have grown to realize that being fully persuaded in God brings a level of trust in what He is doing in and for our lives. If Abraham was not fully convinced that he would become the father of many nations, then we would not be full beneficiaries of the promise. Being fully persuaded is a level that I am growing toward daily. I can remember a time when I was having problems on my job (this is one of the major places the devil attacks me) and God spoke to me and stated that there was going to be a massive firing before He would move me out of my job situation. I was fully persuaded that it was the voice of the devil. I felt that God did not work in that fashion. As the day progressed, I continued to hear that same phrase in my mind, "There is going to be a massive firing before I move you." A month later, those words that God had spoken to me came to pass. Several managers and other personnel were fired for embezzlement of funds and God promoted me. I did not understand the promise He was speaking over my life, but time brought the spoken words to pass. God sometimes has a strange way of speaking to us, but we can rest assured that what He speaks will come to pass. Our father, Abraham (father of faith), is a prime example to every believer that we should learn to speak the language of God, not speaking in doubt, but being fully persuaded that He will perform what He has promised.

Chapter 14

Using Authority Over Criticism

"And as the ark of the Lord came into the city of David, Michal, Saul's daughter, looked through a window, and saw King David leaping and dancing before the Lord; and she despised him in her heart" (2 Samuel 6:16).

"Then David returned to bless his household. And Michal the daughter of Saul came out to meet David, and said, How glorious was the king of Israel today, who uncovered himself today in the eyes of the handmaids of his servants, as one of the vain fellows shamelessly uncovereth himself! And David said unto Michal, It was before the Lord, which chose me before thy father, and before all his house, to appoint me ruler over the people of the Lord, over Israel: therefore will I play before the Lord" (2 Samuel 6:20-21).

Criticism is a word that many of us are familiar with, either from being criticized or from criticizing others. It takes its meaning from the root word critic or being strongly judged. The very act of criticism can be constructive or destructive. Constructive criticism is the act of judging a person's performance with a descriptive eye in hopes that the performance can become better. Contrary to constructive criticism, destructive criticism is done to assassinate one's character and self-worth.

Displayed either way, criticism can be hard. I have found out that it is not very pleasant to the ears of the one being critiqued. It takes a strong personality to accept what others have to say about their character or performance. I am also persuaded that constructive criticism is more easily accepted than destructive. Many times people are not expressing harm when they offer constructive criticism. However, the way it is received has a great bearing on how we react to the person giving the criticism.

In this chapter, I am led to focus directly on destructive criticism rather than constructive. I am assured that many believers do not understand how to cope when this type of action is being displayed. I am not saying that I know everything about this subject, but I have been exposed to some effects of destructive criticism and it can be devastating if we do not understand how it should be handled.

How should we deal with destructive criticism? Can it really be overthrown? These questions and others I feel can be best answered through biblical example.

The main Scriptures from 2 Samuel 6:16, 20-21 of the same chapter displays a very descriptive view of destructive criticism. It displays a spiritual but yet a humanistic approach to this topic. King David had just defeated the Philistines in battle and as a result, the Ark of the Covenant was returned to His native land. It was symbolic of the presence of the Lord and was very sentimental, just as the money was to the woman in the parable of the lost coin (Luke 15:8-10). This not only was a time of victory for the Children of Israel, but it was also a celebration, reuniting the Ark of the Covenant with the correct owners.

King David was so excited about the Ark that he began to offer sacrifices to the Lord as a token of thanksgiving. David began to kill oxen and fatlings (vs. 13) and then proceeded to dance before the

Lord. David's dancing was another way of glorifying God for the finding of the Ark.

David was so consumed with praise and thanksgiving that he danced out of his linen ephod (vs.14 and 20). He was not ashamed to give God praise for what was done for them. Instead, he displayed a public profession for a symbolic expression (the Ark of the Covenant). David knew that there should be a measure of honor given to the One whose presence is forever with us.

The alarming factor to any joyous story is that everyone does not want to join in on the celebration. Many people do not want to have joy when we are joyful, and do not want to express glee when we are gleeful. This is one of the keys to overcoming negative criticism. We must realize that everyone is not going to rally around us when doing things God's way. This is the same dilemma with which King David was faced.

King Saul's daughter, Michal had a hidden agenda behind all the 'I love yous' to King David. The Scripture bears record that "she despised him in her heart" (vs. 16). Can you imagine living with someone, telling them all your secrets and all of your concerns, only to find out that they were all lies? It hurts.

It should be mentioned that destructive criticism is a seed that is planted in the heart. It may start out as an insignificant thought and gradually evil thoughts begin to prevail. One of the main points that we need to consider when dealing with destructive criticism is the heart of the person. We must watch a person's motives to see if they are really destructive or constructive. Sometimes the person may be trying to help us, but we take it the wrong way.

Michal was not the type that would offer constructive criticism. Her motives were wrong. She should have been the one to offer positive thoughts. However, she was becoming the villain in the Davidic household. In this particular case, Michal is symbolic of the enemy. She was there to try and hinder the progress of pleasing God, just as the enemy does today.

Verse 20 states, "Then David returned to bless his household. And Michal the daughter of Saul came out to meet David, and said, 'How glorious was the king of Israel today, who uncovered himself today in the eyes of the handmaids of his servants, as one of the vain fellows shamelessly uncovereth himself!'"

This is where the actual manifestation of the criticism began to flourish, but the initial act was done in the heart. The devil is aware of words. He knows that many lives can be destroyed because of negative words. This is where Michal thought she could gain victory over her husband. If she could lower his self-esteem, she could lower the king. What people think about themselves is an indication of what they can become. And in David's case, he was a prized king.

This is how it should be in every believer's life. You have got to be strong spiritually and mentally to overcome the negative forces of criticism. I am a witness that the devil will use every weakness that you have to try and take you out. Therefore, you must be strong in the Lord.

I remember being in elementary school where the kids would laugh and talk about me because I had a speech impediment. I would say the word pray for the word play. I was a laughingstock to them. Little did they know that God would use that for my good. I did not know how to handle the criticism. I would retaliate by fighting and cursing.

I would cry and even go into hiding. But those methods only got me into a deeper hole. So I remained calm and took it. Just imagine an 8-to-10-year-old just taking criticism. As I pass through my old neighborhood and see those same kids, they now look at me differently. It was not that I knew how to control them, but it was my standing still and allowing God to fight for me that allowed me to overcome the criticism.

Verses 21-22 offer the main keys through which David overcame his criticism. "And David said unto Michal, 'It was before the Lord, which chose me before thy father, and before all his house, to appoint me ruler over the people of the Lord, over Israel: therefore will I play before the Lord. And I will yet be viler than thus, and will be base in mine own sight: and of the maidservants which thou hast spoken of, and of them shall I be had in honor.'"

David allowed his authority to step in when he stated his purpose for dancing. Purpose is the supreme key to overcoming destructive criticism. He said, "It was before the Lord." He was not concerned about anything else but the Lord. Although Michal was his wife, the Lord was the most important. This is the attitude all believers must take. Learn to please the Lord. David was bold with this statement. This was very simple phrasing but carried much spiritual weight. This is why the Scripture states that God uses the foolish or the small things of the world to confound the wise.

We must remember our purpose. Purpose feeds our inner man and causes a deep determination for ministry. Purpose also forces us to forget the degrading comments of others and places us on a plane of focus. Many times our authority is not utilized because of a lack of purpose. We are not acutely aware of what is our main priority, "This is where the security of who we are comes into play. We should not be concerned about what men say about us, as long as we are aware that God knows our purpose; that is all that counts.

Verse 21 also houses a very good point worthy of mentioning, that is, we must be aware of where we originate. David said, "It was before the Lord which chose me before thy father, and before all his house, to appoint me ruler over the people of the Lord, over Israel: therefore will I play before the Lord." Although Saul chose David, God chose him first. In other words, David could not be bought or sold. He was a descendant of a higher power. Therefore, David could speak with authority. This is a lesson for us. Although you may be under someone's authority or someone allowed you to be promoted to a higher position, know that if you are a child of God, you are still bound by a higher standard. If God tells you to speak a godly Word to your boss, you are held accountable to do so. If you begin to offer praise in places where you normally do not frequent, remember, it is better to obey God than to obey man.

I am not saying that we should disregard the authority of others, but when God is leading one to do a specific task, it is of utmost importance that we heed His commands. This is the same attitude the earlier apostle displayed.

Finally, in verses 21-22, David began to give his final comments to Michal. After counting all the cost and making a bold stance, David emerged with an attitude of confidence. He stated, "...therefore will I play before the Lord. And I will yet be viler than thus, and will be base in mine own sight..." Some people may declare this statement as being boastful, or high-minded, and even arrogant. However, this was not the case. David was expressing his confidence over the criticism.

These verses also bring into light our final point. Do not allow destructive criticism to change your lifestyle. Many times we change our habits, our ways, methods, or worship styles because of destructive criticism. I have heard of some churches where people are not allowed to express their feelings toward God. They cannot say thank you Lord, Hallelujah, or even praise the Lord. This is a type of bondage and it goes against the teachings of the Scripture. God specifically says in His Word, "Let the redeemed of the Lord say so, whom he hath redeemed from the hand of the enemy" (Psalm 107:2). This is a command of God. God uses the word let as a sign of command that this is to be done.

I can remember a time when I was prompted by the Holy Spirit to express a testimony. I began to look around at the people and I became afraid of what they would say to me. A dear friend approached me after the service and stated that she knew that I was supposed to testify. She also told me not to be afraid to express what God had done in my life. This was a release. I learned from that moment not to allow myself to be placed in bondage.

David was of the same persuasion. He took a bold stance and proclaimed that he would continue to praise the Lord despite his wife's opinion.

However, If we are to utilize our authority, we should not let our lives revolve around what someone else thinks about our expressions to God. If you are bothered by the statements of others, ask God for guidance. Do not just yield to destructive criticism. If you are thoroughly convinced that God has called you to a specific task, then go with God.

Chapter 15
Authoritative Weapons

"Put on the whole armour of God, that ye may be able to stand against the wiles of the devil." Ephesians 6:11

"Wherefore take unto you the whole armor of God that ye may be able to withstand in the evil day, and having done all, to stand. Stand therefore, having your loins girt about with truth, and having on the breastplate of righteousness; And your feet shod with the preparation of the gospel of peace; Above all, taking the shield of faith, wherewith ye shall be able to quench all the fiery darts of the wicked. And take the helmet of salvation, and the sword of the Spirit, which is the Word of God. "Ephesians 6:13-17

We are enlisted in the Christian Army. And being in this army requires that we utilize the weapons given to us. These spiritual weapons are the offensive and defensive devices needed to counteract the enemy's attacks. These weapons are a must for the believer. Moreover, we cannot afford not to have on this armor. It is one of our protective coverings. It is one of the Christian's life-support suits.

As stated in prior chapters, it is our duty to occupy until Christ returns for us, His bride. In the interim, we must labor for the faith. He has delegated this duty to no other agent but His church. More fascinating, Christ would not leave His property without protection. He stated in John 14:14, "And I will pray the Father, and he shall give you another Comforter, that he may abide with you forever." The Holy Spirit is our comforter or from the Greek translation "Parakletos" (our advocate).

Paul also instructs us in the Word that God has given us an undressable armor. Ephesians 6:11 tells us to "Put on the whole armor of God, that ye may be able to stand against the wiles of the devil." The Scripture never tells us to take off the armor once it is put on. This armor is to be worn forever by the believer. This suggests that we should be constantly on guard against the attacks of the enemy. If our armor is not securely fastened, then the enemy may strike us with one of his weapons.

When the armor is worn, we must do a routine maintenance to see if it is up to par. The way we do routine checks is by studying the Word of God, praying, fellowshipping with other saints, and proclaiming the truth of the Word. The Holy Spirit will inform you if you are not operating the way you should. However, routine check-ups allow our armor to be in constant operation so that we will not be defeated when we go into battle.

Another thought-provoking point that should be mentioned is that this armor was delegated to the believer by God. Verse 11 says that it is "of God." This armor is the essence of God's character and holiness. It speaks of who He is and what He stands for. God longs to see His people secured in peace and in safety. Therefore, the armor is an emblem and mirror of God, And when we put on the armor, we are putting on Him.

Whole, Not Part

For many years I have heard the expression "part of a whole." It may have been in mathematics class or in some area of geometry. The expression is true. We can have part of a whole.

How does this relate to the believer's uniform? Many times we are accustomed to making use of part of the armor and not the full. This causes us to fight half-suited. When officers go into battle, they make sure that they have on all pieces of their uniform. This allows them to be well-equipped when going into battle. This is the same concept in regard to the whole armor of God. We are sufficiently assured when we have on "whole and not part" of the armor. Each piece of the armor works together. They work in complete harmony with each other. They are a system of checks and balances. They exist to aid each other.

I remember talking to a fellow church member. He was in between jobs and he stated that he liked being a "floater" and not being able to receive the full benefits of the job. The Holy Spirit spoke to me to say to him, "Why should we accept part of a blessing when the whole is waiting to be used." He then shook his head in agreement.

This is how God wants us to view the armor of God. It is the whole that makes the greatest impact rather than the part. Learn how to think whole-minded and not part-minded. When we allow this mind set to take priority, then we truly are operating in the authority God has set for us.

The Believer's Uniform

Many of us are familiar with Ephesians 6:13-17, which describes each piece of the believer's armor. This Scripture has been talked about, preached, recited, and recounted in a number of settings. I also think it is necessary to discuss these pieces again in detail. I do believe that repetition is good for us. It causes an individual to get the meaning embedded in his or her mind and heart. Below you will find descriptions of each authoritative armor piece and why it is so important.

Loins girt with truth. This piece of armor is a foundational piece that allows the believer to take a firm stance. The loins in the natural sense are the part of the body between the side and the back that holds the pelvis in place. Spiritually speaking, the loins girt with truth exists symbolically for the believer to be alert and ready for active duty. This piece of armor is the basis for the believer's profession of Christ. Just like the natural belts that we use to keep our clothing intact, the loins are to be held in place with the belt of truth. It is the truth of the Word of God on which we should stand. Vines Expository Dictionary records that a believer's loins girt about with truth is a place of generative power. This is a place where we as believers bring our authority into existence. Our authority is based upon the truth of God's Word. This is how we operate, unlike our enemy who operates with deceit and trickery. When we gird our loins, we are on the way toward victory.

Breastplate of righteousness. Along with the loins being girt with truth, there exists another piece of armor that deals with our integrity. The integrity of the believer is that of honesty and moral conduct. Integrity simply is the character of the believer. However, the breastplate protects the believer from being violated of his integrity. When a believer is persecuted by the use of lies, slander, and character attacks, the breastplate repels the accusations and leaves us robed in righteousness. The breastplate in biblical times was a piece of metal that covered the chest, back, and neck areas of the soldier. It protected the warrior from being injured in vital areas such as the heart and throat. What does this say about the spiritual armor? The breastplate guards our heart from the emotional traumas of the enemy. He may throw a spiritual javelin at the heart of the believer, but it is guarded by the breastplate.

Many people have said that the covering for the back was not mentioned in this portion of the Scripture. As stated earlier, the back was also guarded by the breastplate. This is exciting to know when we are facing the enemy, that even our backs are covered. The enemy cannot do any harm to us from the back because God also has our back (He is protecting us).

Feet shod with the Gospel of Peace; The Bible teaches us that we should live peaceably with all mankind. It is our duty to walk in a realm of peace. When it comes to shodding our feet with the Gospel of peace, it is primarily telling us to always have a readiness to proclaim the Word of God to all mankind. It is the believer's responsibility to bring peace to a confused world. When we bear the Good News of Jesus Christ, we are bringing peace to troubled lands.

The Gospel of Jesus Christ is a peaceful Gospel. It is not one that brings turmoil or confusions, but peace. However, true peace is an atmosphere only brought about by the Word of God. It is not brought about through peace talks or world conventions. It is the Word of God that binds men and nations. Wherever we are and whatever we do, we should always be prepared to bring peace with us. After all, it is part of our spiritual makeup (Gal. 5:22).

Shield of Faith - The Bible states in Ephesians 6:16, "Above all taking the shield of faith wherewith you are able to quench all the fiery darts of the wicked." Why does the Bible place high priority on the shield of faith? Why is faith important? In order for the believer to walk in the authority of God, it is most important for him to trust in his main protection.

When we trust in God, He hovers over as a hen hovers over her brood. He covers the total of us. To better understand the shield of faith, I feel that it is important for us to discuss some regarding the biblical warrior's shield. The shield was not a shield as we know it today. It was a much larger shield that covered the majority of the body. The warrior became more dependent upon the shield to cover the entire body, rather than the individual parts. This is the same type of principle that is applied to the shield of faith. Our main shield is our faith, that is, the faith in God Who indwells us. Through Him we can lift our shield to quench or deter all the missiles that the enemy tries to launch. Faith is the ground by which the believer lives. It is the potency for our walk. Faith is the portal by which our prayers are answered. It is because of faith that we now live a consecrated life. I want to admonish each of you today, continue to lift your faith when the wicked one tries to override your authority. Remember, you are in the position of authority. You are the one that can dispel the enemy's darts, And most of all, remember that your victory comes through your shield faith.

Helmet of Salvation. The helmet of salvation is a safety device. It is a safeguard for the mind. Many biblical warriors often wore helmets to protect themselves from weapons attacking their head. They knew that if the head was out of balance the whole body would be also. So it is with the spiritual. The helmet serves to protect you and me from the weapons of doubt that the enemy devises. He may use a nagging thought to try and destroy the balance that the Word of God gives. He may even use a forgiven sin to detour your thought pattern. Nevertheless, God has given us the helmet which serves as a repellent against the devil's instruments. The helmet works by the believer constantly filling the thought patterns with the Word of God. The Holy Spirit then seals the Word and causes it to be retrieved when the attacks come. Although the believer does not see the helmet, it is there working on his behalf. Moreover, the helmet works in conjunction with the breastplate which protects the heart (emotions, feelings). The helmet controls the thoughts being filtered into the heart. It functions to cast out thoughts that go contrary to the Word of God. Not only is it our thought navigator, but our thought protector.

Sword of the Spirit -Throughout history, swords have been weapons of defense. They served to counteract the attacks of the enemy. So it is with the Word of God. The sword represents the defense of the Word of God on our behalf. The Word is ready to avenge all attacks devised by our enemies. So many times in my life, I did not know that the Word of God was my defensive and offensive weapon. Instead, I would stand around worrying about how I would handle the problems that I had encountered. So often, we only view the Word of God as an uplifting book and seldom view it as our defense. This is where we are held in bondage. The Word of God not only uplifts, it also defends.

The Word of God is not dull. It has a cutting-edge power unlike any other sword. Not only is the Word powerful, it has a way of penetrating areas beyond our wildest imagination. It discerns the thoughts and intents of our hearts (Hebrews 4:12). There must be training for the warrior when using a sword. He may learn the characteristics of the sword, deal with the sword's weight and then he may go through a series of tests. He may cut down some bushes or small shrubs to see the impact that the sword makes. What I am trying to say? If you and I are going to be effective in utilizing the authority of the Word, we must learn how to train with it. Your training may be a small battle that you are going through or it may be from studying. But whatever the case may be, learn to be skillful in the Word of God. For the Word is our spiritual sword.

Praise in Action

"And when he had consulted with the people, he appointed singers unto the Lord, and that should praise the beauty of holiness, as they went out before the army, and to say, Praise the Lord; for his mercy endureth forever. And when they began to sing and to praise, the Lord set ambushments against the children of Ammon Moab, and Mount Seir, which were come against Judah; and they were smitten." 2 Chronicles. 20:21-22

Praise—our garment against hopelessness, depression, despair, and persecution is a most powerful weapon. It is an area in which we have allowed our spiritual understanding to slip. It is through praise that we become ushered into the presence of God. It is because of praise that joy returns to its rightful owner. Many times we have placed more emphasis on the weapon of prayer than the other tools needed to live an abundant life. This is not to discredit the power and fervency of prayer. It is much needed, So often we fail to remember that we need spiritual balance. We sometimes allow our side of our lives to be heavily weighted by one spiritual component and neglect all others. We need both prayer and praise. They are inseparable twins. We cannot function without either.

What is praise? Praise is simply boasting about the goodness of God through word or deed. Praise from God's people is a way of expressing a sincere gratitude to God. It is a way that we transfer the expressions given to us from men to credit the One who is supreme. I remember receiving accolades from several people for winning awards and events. They really made me feel good, but I knew that the true praise should be given to God. It is during moments such as these that we allow the authority of praise to take root in our lives. I could have easily gotten caught up in the moment of celebration and become haughty, but God allowed a transfer of praise to occur.

What about those times of discouragement and stress? How can praise work for us? Although anyone can praise the Lord (Psalm 150:6), I feel that praise is especially a universal weapon for the believer. It can work through the good and bad times in our lives. The way in which we make use of praise is where we fall short. Many believers are ineffective with this weapon. Some regard praise as a Sunday worship duty, but not a daily life issue. Praise should be a minute-by-minute, day-by-day, and a year-by-year affair. When we take this attitude to heart then we are a step away from walking in total victory.

Praise can be seen in the main Scripture reference with the children of Israel and their enemies. The twentieth chapter of 2 Chronicles, foretells the invasion of Moab against the tribe of Judah. Judah was a very fortified city and God had given it to them (vs. 11). It was told to King Jehoshaphat that the children of Moab were steadily approaching. Consequently, King Jehoshaphat began to fear (vs. 3). Many of us might think that this is a response of a coward, but this is not so. I am of the persuasion that fear is a natural process to the flesh when there is mind-boggling news at a moment's notice. This causes a reaction to the flesh. The flesh becomes out of control. Hands become sweaty. The heart begins to pound, but the Spiritual man is not bothered, only the flesh. This is the reason Apostle Paul says that "I [the Holy Spirit indwelling us] keep under my body and bring it [flesh] into subjection..." (I Corinthians 9:27). So do not become overwhelmed with fear, but allow the Holy Spirit to keep you focused.

Although King Jehoshaphat was fearful, his spiritual nature retreated to other means. He began to seek the Lord and made a declarative fast throughout the land (vs.3). This is kingly authority now speaking in Jehoshaphat. There will come a time when the kings and priests in you will rise to even greater degrees. You will begin to speak and act like a king should act. You will begin to say and do things that go against your natural process.

Can you imagine the children of Judah encamped around their leader saying, "What are we going to do?" They were frantic, feeble and most of all in fear. This is the same episode that transpired with Moses and the children of Israel during their Red Sea era. The only answer that was fitting for King Jehoshaphat's pressing dilemma was to seek the face of God through prayer (vs. 4-13). Praise is interwoven in prayer. As stated earlier, you cannot separate the two. In the process of prayer, praise stirs the heart of God. It romances God. It makes God feel really good. The Word of God instructs us that "God inhabits the praises of His people (Psalms 22:3). He delights when we praise him, and it is where he dwells—in our praise.

Praise through prayer causes us to acknowledge the very nature of God. We then find ourselves saying as Jehoshaphat in his prayer to God, "O Lord God of our fathers, art not thou God in heaven? And rules not thou over all the kingdoms of the heathen? and in thine hand is there not power and might, so that none is able to withstand thee?" (2 Chronicles 20:6). King Jehoshaphat praised God through prayer by expressing that He is the God that rules everything. At this point, he touched God's sovereignty. He touched the very essence of who God is. This is how we excite God. Sincere praise lets God know that we are serious about matters. It illuminates and magnifies God and humbles us. And when this is done, we are displaying praise in action.

Giving praise to God is not a natural process to the carnal mind. It takes a spiritual mind set to enter into the presence of God. It forces you and me out of our comfort zones into a place of total reliance on God. This is what King Jehoshaphat had to realize. Before any of God's children expects a mighty move from God, they must prepare their mind to receive what God is saying about release. This is why praise is so important. It prunes the heart. It calms every doubt. It causes one's soul to be in complete harmony with heaven. I know this may sound bizarre, but I do believe that spiritual breakthroughs come through bizarre measures. If we are going to become skilled with using the authority of praise, we must learn to get out of ourselves and focus on God. We must learn not to focus on the nagging job, the disobedient child, the non-committed wife or husband or any area in our life and we must focus on God.

"And when they began to sing and to praise, the Lord set ambushments against the children of Amman, Moab, and mount Seir, which were come against Judah; and they were smitten" (2 Chronicles 20:22).

Time is of the essence. It causes the very things that we have no control over to be placed into their rightful state. I can hear the wisdom of my mom saying, "Just wait on time." It was not until I began to grow in God that this saying was awakened. There are moments in a believer's life in which time is the only tool that brings us closer to God. In circumstance after circumstance, trial after trial, we find through time that God is needed.

Judah was in a pressing situation. Time was of the essence. They could not depend on anyone to deliver them but God. Have you ever had a "but-God experience?" The enemies in your life were steadily approaching and you had no other alternatives. You began to go to those who you thought were in authority (not even mindful of your own authority). And to your dismay, you were still caught between a rock and hard place. Somewhere in the back of your mind, you began to think, I have tried everything except God.

God instructed Judah not to fight in this battle and that God would be the one doing the fighting (2 Chronicles 20:16). Can you imagine the flesh calling out to Judah as the enemies were approaching? The hands begin to shake and the heart begins to pulsate to a level that is truly unreal. Many of us can identify with this scenario. Your situation may not be that of a physical enemy coming to your doorstep, but the enemy may be in the back room of your thoughts. The enemy may be saying, "It's time for you to give up. You have run out of time and there is no one that can help you." Do not allow those thoughts to penetrate your spirit. It can cause utter depression. This is the time when we need to allow the praise of God to overtake us. The very function of praise is that it drives away heaviness, that is depression, oppression, and any type of bondage that causes a dreary spirit to overshadow us (Isaiah 61:3).

In 2 Chronicles 20:22 states, "And when they began to sing and to praise, the Lord set ambushments against the children of Amman, Moab, and Mount Seir, which were come against Judah; and they were smitten."

As the enemy was approaching, the Israelites may have heard the beat of the enemy's drums. The Israelites may have heard their war cries and even seen the elaborate armor that they wore. But something happened when Judah began to sing and to praise. Their enemies were destroyed. This is where the pulse of praise begins to flourish. As they opened their mouths and began to sing, "Praise the Lord, for his mercy endureth forever" victory came to life. It was not that their voices were so sweet and pleasing to the ear, but it was because praise came out of a sincere and true heart. It is amazing what a gospel song or a song of praise can do to the heart of God and also the believer. Have you ever been depressed and it seems as if you could not come out of it. But somewhere in your heart there was song of praise.

Praise is a spiritual force that pulls God's people out of dungeon situations. You may have the enemies at your doorstep and you may even be listening to a frightening voice, but I declare that if you open your mouth and sing a song of praise, deliverance will come.

The pulse of praise can be compared to the human heart which contracts and causes beating in the arteries. When the brain senses a bit of tension and stress, the heart rate has a tendency to pulsate. Judah's praise caused God's heart to contract and to move on their behalf when He saw Judah's sincerity. This is the reason the Bible tells us that they that worship him must worship Him in spirit and in truth (John 4:24). Judah's praise started the pulse of God's war arm to move quickly. Every note that Judah uttered was a strike against the enemy. Every compassionate beat from their heart was a cord that caressed the heart of God and every melody that was expressed was a sign of their deepest adoration to God.

Judah was truly doing what they knew best. When King Jehoshaphat appointed singers before the Lord (2 Chronicles 20:21) it was not by chance. As we study biblical genealogy, we can see that Judah had a nature to praise. In Genesis 29:16-35, is where we first learn of Judah's pulse of praise. As the story unfolds, we see Jacob, after stealing the birthright, goes to live with his Uncle Laban for fear of his life. There Jacob asks to marry Laban's daughter, Rachel, who was young and beautiful. Jacob agreed to work for Laban seven years and was to marry Rachel after this period. Time had expired and Jacob asked for Rachel's hand in marriage. Laban agreed but had a hidden agenda. Laban tricked Jacob by giving him his oldest daughter, Leah, who was not very pleasing to the eye. Jacob married Leah as well as Rachel. However, Jacob loved Rachel more than Leah and this act vexed the heart of God. As a result of Leah being hated, God opened her womb and blessed her and gave her four sons (Reuben, Simeon, Levi, and Judah). There was something strange about the fourth child Judah. The fourth son was a representation of gratitude that God had shown to her. Therefore she called him Judah, which means praise. Leah said in verse 23, "Now will I praise the Lord: therefore she called his name Judah; and left bearing."

We can see that praise was pulsated from birth. This is why God's heart was touched when Judah began to praise Him before their enemies. God remembered the agony, the ridicule and the hatred Leah suffered. Not only was the suffering remembered, but also the pulsated praise that Leah uttered.

There is a strange phenomenon that happens to a believer when experiencing ridicule and suffering—the believer begins to offer to God a deeper praise. The believer realizes that the part of him that is wounded can be healed when entering into praise. The wound may be a reminder that you are still in pain. However, I want you to know that the wound does not have to be a reminder of pain, guilt, or any condemnation. It can stand for victory.

I remember one of the battles that I endured which did leave some painful scars. The ulcers in my chest are a reminder of the battle that I endured. God had to teach me through the pulse of praise that those wounds could be conquered. I had to learn to utter praise to God even when the ulcers were striking blows against my chest. I would get into a quiet room and meditate and sing songs of deliverance to

God. The major pains decreased, but I am still believing God for a full recovery. Not only am I being delivered from physical pain---my memory has been healed of negative thoughts. Every time I come in contact with the people who caused me agony, I can now smile and say, "I gained the victory through my praise to God."

Since God does not suffer from spiritual amnesia, God is still remembering the pulse of praise. He still remembers Judah. Saints, we are now the spiritual Judah because we have been adopted by Jesus Christ, who came through the linage of Judah. Although we may have different ethnic backgrounds, nationalities and praise styles---we are the praise of God.

Chapter 16
The Authority of Prayer

"If my people, which are called by my name, shall humble themselves, and pray, and seek my face, and turn from their wicked ways; then will I hear from heaven, and will forgive their sins, and will heal their lands 2 Chronicles 7:14.

I could not finish this book without including a section on prayer. E. M. Bounds, a noted preacher and evangelist said, "The neglect of prayer is a token of dead spiritual desires." It behooves each of us who believes in prayer to pray unceasingly.

Prayer is the believer's vehicle of communication to the Heavenly Father. It is through prayer that we touch the heart of God and receive what we ask for. The Bible clearly says in St. Mark 11:24, "…what things soever ye desire, when you pray, believe that ye receive them, and ye shall have them." Our desires, requests, and petitions must be submitted through the vehicle of prayer. It is by no other supernatural medium that requests are granted for believers.

The main Scripture reference, 2 Chronicles 7:14, has been quoted and used on a number of occasions and rightly so. It bespeaks the various needs of spiritual break-throughs in society today. If there ever was a time that prayer needs to be manifested by believers it is now. We have experienced a generation of wasted talent, gifts, ideas, and values because the majority of the Christian community is not praying. This is a very bold statement for me to make, but the above Scripture says, "If my people…" This suggests to me that it is inclusive of the entire body of Christ coming together and praying that things change.

As stated earlier, God did not leave the responsibility to change the world to anyone but the Church. This is where the authority of the believer comes into play. For too long, we as Christians have allowed perverse things to happen in our streets, neighborhoods, and world. Why? The Church is not a weak body of believers that cannot exercise power and authority over issues that plague our world. We have been endowed with a source of power that can overthrow any evil force. However, we, as members of the body of Christ, must recognize the spiritual tools that God has invested in us.

I can recall the years that the entire nation gathered together in prayer for the U.S. Troops in the Middle East. People of all walks of life came, repented, and prayed that the situation would be resolved and it happened. What happened to that same synergy of prayer? Was it just a point of showmanship? Today, we need that same fervor and authority that was manifested during war time.

Jesus, in Matthew 18:18, tells us that we have the power and the authority to bind (or to bring into subjection) anything that we desire when we come united in prayer. He stands there backing us. We have been delegated the right and privilege to stand in agreement believing that whatever we pray for will come to pass (according to God's time frame).

That is the reason why 2 Chronicles 7:14 expresses the view that we are called by His name, that is, we have the backing of the one whose name is honored in heaven. Is that not wonderful to know that God in heaven is there waiting to answer our prayers?

I am convinced that the authority of prayer is a realm of belief that some people have failed to lay hold to. We need to continue to believe that what we have prayed for will be granted. So often we grow uneasy when our prayers do not get answered instantaneously. But the authority of prayer tells us to stand in faith, believing for what we have prayed.

If prayer is going to be effective and spoken with authority, one must truly believe that what was spoken from the heart will come to pass. This is where the problem lies with the effectiveness and fervency of prayer. Some believers are not radical in their petitions to God. Radical prayer leads to radical results. This view is backed by Abraham in Romans 4 when he radically believed God for the promise that God had made to him.

Romans 4:19-21, states, "And being not weak in faith, he considered not his own body now dead, when he was about an hundred years old, neither yet the deadness of Sarah's womb: He staggered not at the promise of God through unbelief, but was strong in faith, giving glory to God; and being fully persuaded that, what he had promised, he was able also to perform."

Although this Scripture does not point out the fact that Abraham prayed, it speaks of his unwavering belief in God. This is what prayer is truly about: faith. Abraham was actually radical enough to believe God for the things that were promised to him. How much more can we do since we are now the sons and daughters of Abraham?

I dare not let my memory pass me by as to my use of the authority of prayer. During the summer of 1997, our youth group took a trip to Deland, FL, to do mission work. We were to go and minister to kids and adults who were physically and mentally challenged. Upon our arrival, we took a tour of the campsite where we would stay for the time and there was much to be desired. The young people went into culture shock. The lodges were made of wood, no air conditioning, cracks in the floors and the constant torment of flying squirrels and crawling lizards. And to top it off, the youth were complaining about the 100 degree heat in the lodges. I began to tell the youth supervisors that I would not complain and would lie down and pray that God would send rain.

I prayed and the constant comments of the kids came to mind. I began to think about Moses when the Israelites were complaining about being brought into the wilderness to die. I prayed, "Lord, in the Name of Jesus, please allow a multitude of rain to come and cool the campsite. Please manifest Your power in a mighty way." And within a span of an hour, rain came pouring out of the sky and continued for a couple of hours, after which, a rainbow appeared. I was convinced that God had answered my prayer and the attitudes of the youth were changed to thankfulness. Thank God for the authority of prayer.

Six Conditions of Authoritative Prayer

In order for prayer to be authoritative, there are some conditions that the believer has to follow. God has revealed six conditions that will be beneficial to believers as prayers continue to be uttered.

Condition One: We Must Have A Relationship

Prayer must be that tie that binds the believer with the heart of God. This is the period where the believer comes into sweet communion with God and discloses his innermost thoughts and concerns. It is at this point that the believer becomes intimate with God and a deeper relationship is formed.

Prayer should be the type of communication in which the believer knows what he wants and desires and God understands him and the desire. That is why a relationship is so important when it comes to prayer.

Prayer is a supernatural component and the unbeliever does not understand it because there is no relationship established. The Bible clearly bears record of this in I Corinthians 2:14. Prayer is considered foolishness to the unregenerate man and he cannot know spiritual things until he becomes regenerated (born-again).

I recall seeing billboards saying, "A family that prays together stays together." I agree with the philosophy behind the theme. However, all families do not have a relationship with Christ. Therefore, God does not hear the family's prayers. I have come to the conclusion, that a believer should not tell someone to pray when they do not know the spiritual condition of that person. The first thing that needs to be done is to assess if the person has accepted Jesus Christ. If the person is not saved, try to be instrumental in leading the person to a relationship with Christ.

Furthermore, God does not hear the prayer of a believer when he regards iniquity in his heart (Psalm 66:18). Sin has a way of hindering the believers' sincere prayers from being answered. Sin places a dark cloud between the believer and God, thereby, causing a breach in fellowship. Notice, I said the fellowship and not the relationship. I will forever be God's son and He my father, but our fellowship can be broken.

In order for our prayers to be effective and authoritative, we must deal with sin and not allow it to overtake us. We must know beyond any doubt that we have a relationship and are in fellowship with Christ.

These revelations are important components that we must know in order to be effective in the craft of prayer.

Condition Two: Don't Think of Prayer as Saying Mere Words

Too often we allow ourselves to be tangled in the "wordiness" of prayer. Prayer is not saying mere words. Words in prayer are the agents that express the direct feelings from our heart to God's throne room. Words are powerful. They are the tools to change our destiny. Proverbs 18:21 teaches that the power of life and death is in the tongue. What we begin to say out of our mouths can speak life or death to our circumstances.

So it is with prayer. The words that we utter to God are not plain words. They are the substance to change areas in our lives. I do believe that the reason some of our prayers are not answered is because of our approach to prayer. We cannot approach prayer with the view of saying mere words. We must use the approach that our words are catalysts that excite God to move on our behalf.

In 2 Kings 19:14-19 lay a great example of the use of words in prayer. King Hezekiah had received a threatening letter from Sennacherib stating that he would overtake the land and defy the Almighty God. Hezekiah went into prayer, and, taking the letter, he laid it before the Lord. Below is part of his prayer:

"O Lord God of Israel, which dwells between the cherubims thou art the God, even thou alone, of all the kingdoms of the earth; thou has made heaven and earth. Lord, bow down thine ear, and hear: open, Lord, thine eye, and see: and hear the words of Sennacherib, which hath sent him to reproach the living God" (vs. 15-16).

Hezekiah's prayer was one that spoke specifically to the heart of the matter. His words in this prayer were very fitting. He knew the problem and directly related his concerns to God. Although Hezekiah was very eloquent in his prayer, he knew the power of words. He knew how to get the attention of God, not out of urgency alone, but by the sincerity of his words.

Condition Three: Must Be a Sincere And Humble Prayer

When prayer and people are not sincere, then the prayer ceases to be prayer. It simply becomes rhetoric. God is seeking the hearts of people who are sincere and humble. Sincerity and humbleness are the characteristics that give fervor and power to prayer. God not only hears the prayer, but sees the person behind the prayer. This is very important for us to keep in mind.

Jesus, in Luke 18:9-14 uses the perfect parable to describe the types of prayers that are honored or rejected by heaven. The pharisee prayed, "God, I thank thee, that I am not as other men are, extortioners, unjust, adulterers, or even as this publican. I fast twice in the week, I give tithes of all that I possess." And the publican prayed, "God, be merciful to me a sinner."

These two prayers show us the character of people. Many times we have a tendency to pray just like the Pharisee with a deep degree of arrogance and this hinders us from reaching the throne room of prayer. Prayer should not express our ability to God, but his ability toward us. Whenever a true believer in Jesus Christ approaches prayer, he detaches himself from his abilities and capabilities and focuses on the one who is the giver of life.

The publican, on the other hand, shows a believer the right way to approach God. He says, "Be merciful to me, a sinner." What he is truly conveying is "Lord, I am nothing, but I come to you who is everything." This is the way that we should approach God. The publican was not concerned about his ability, his background, or his financial status. He was humbly bowing himself to the almighty God. If all of us would just adopt this view of the publican, prayers can be more potent.

The publican's statement also brings another important point into view. Prayers do not have to be lengthy to be effective. The publican's prayer was six words long, but was moving and effective. We live in a society where some think prayers have to be lengthy to touch God's heart. God is not concerned about the number of words that we use in our prayers. He is concerned about the sincerity behind the prayer. Too often we offer "Pharisee prayers" to make an impression. God is not impressed by these prayers. He is not moved nor does he act on merely eloquent prayers.

Jesus summed up the two prayers by saying that the publican's prayer was more justified than the Pharisee's because the publican knew the power of humility (Author's translation vs. 19). Humility is the key to being effective in anything that we do. Even with our prayers, God assesses them to see if they are representative of humility or arrogance. How are your prayers?

Condition Four: Sealed By Faith

In our church we have a saying: "If you are going to doubt, don't pray. If you are going to pray, don't doubt." I don't know who created this slogan, however, he or she knew about praying in faith Prayer should never be done with an inkling of doubt. This causes the prayer to be ineffective. All prayers must be sealed in faith. We must remember that we are praying to a God that is only moved by our faith. Hebrews 11:6 states that without faith, it is impossible to please God.

Faith in God is the key to our prayers. It is the covering that God has designed for our prayers. Mark 11:24 bears record to this fact, "Therefore I say unto you, What things soever ye desire, when ye pray, believe that ye receive them, and ye shall have them." Believing as this Scripture denotes is the prerequisite for receiving what we pray for.

Condition Five: A Continuation of Praying

An unknown author noted, "Prayer is the key that unlocks the door in the morning and prayer is the key that locks the door at night." Continuous prayer is a way of refreshing the believer. It causes constant communion between the person and God.

Many people often ask the question, "Why should a person continue to pray when God hears all prayers?" Our continuous prayers are not symbolic of the fact that God cannot hear, but it does represent our constant dependency upon God. Prayer in its very nature is one that is centered around the life of believer. Everything that the believer does should be centered around the realm of prayer. The believer should not make a decision on a matter until he or she comes into the convincing power that God answered the prayer. I do believe that if many of us as believers would take the time to develop a habit of prayer, our daily thought process would be better, our concerns would be perfected and our worries would turn into delight. These results display the effectiveness and authority of prayer.

Prayer should not only be continuous because it is a lifestyle, but by the mere act of obedience to the Word of God. God instructs us in I Thessalonians 5:17 to "Pray without ceasing." When a believer comes into the knowledge and power of continuous prayer, he or she is dangerous. Unceasing prayer moves the believer from the infant stage of spirituality to the powerful state of spiritual maturity in Christ. The devil then becomes aware of the fact that the believer is continually being filled with the power of God through his or her prayer life. The devil is also aware of the fact that when a believer spends time alone in prayer with God, a spiritual metamorphoses occurs. This may sound extraordinary, but it is true. There is a sense of clarity that overshadows the believer. He becomes aware of the devil's tactics. However, the devil also becomes acutely aware of those who spend time with God. He knows that his mission is threatened and canceled when constant prayer is made by the believer. This is the reason why he watches you, perplexes you, and tries to intimidate you because he knows that you are a prayer warrior. Continue to pray without ceasing.

Condition Six: Desire in Prayer

As stated in the early portion of the book, "the neglect of prayer is the token of dead spiritual desires." E.M. Bounds is declaring here that when prayers are not intertwined with desire, it ceases to be impactful prayer. The prayer becomes mere words. Desire is a central necessity in the prayer life of the believer. It is the goal of the prayer. Desire is the spark that is being spoken out of the heart when prayers are uttered.

There is something very alarming about desire in our prayers. It provides importunity or a sense of urgency. Psalm 102:17 states, "He will regard the prayer of the destitute, and not despise their prayer." When a believer is at the breaking point in his or her life, God makes a special appointment to remedy their circumstance.

It is not that God only answers stressful or destitute prayers from believers; He merely gives special attention to the intense desire that is being expressed in the prayer.

I can remember times in my life when I needed God to step in immediately. Tears flowed, my mind was perplexed, and faith was low. All I had to do was to fall on my knees and utter my desires to God. God was there. It does not take time for God to react when the desire is sincere. Sincere desires are a treasure to God. He loves to honor prayers backed by the right desires and correct motives.

There is also a flip side to this area of desire in prayer. There are times when the sincere desire exists in our prayers, but God sometimes does not answer the prayer in the fashion that we want him to. I have found out that the creature cannot truly ask or make a demand on the creator. God knows what is best for us. He is uniquely crafting us into the men or women of God that He has destined us to be. Sometimes this means going through the rough times so that character is built. This is not to say that God is dishonoring our desire. He is honoring it, but in a different manner. God has a unique order of operations and we cannot discern it. However, our duty is to pray with sincere desire and it is God's duty to answer the prayer in the manner in which He sees fit.

Final Note

Walking in heavenly authority is a constant effort. We cannot learn how this view works just by reading a book or attending a seminar. It is learned throughout our lives. It is during times of loneliness and distress that God births things out of us that we sometimes do not understand. This is one area in my life that God had to reveal. God has destined His people with the essential tools needed to live victorious lives. However, many of us are not sensitive enough to the Spirit of God and, as a result, we are not skillful with God's Word. That is why it is important for every born again believer to know their rights and privileges in Christ. It is time for us to know who we are in Christ so that we cannot be bound by the enemy's tactics.

There is also an awakening for the believer when he or she comes into the knowledge of their spiritual heritage. As the believer becomes more cautious and more understanding regarding the ways of God, spiritual growth begins to occur, warfare is learned, and a deep awareness of God is truly formed. This is the beauty of the authority of the believer. God longs to see His people delivered from a spiritual state of infancy to a glorious state of maturity in Him. Once we come to the understanding of who Jesus is and who we are in Christ, we are bound by the cords of spiritual authority. We become bold in our spiritual walk because we are assured of our position in Christ.

This book serves as a reminder to all believers of where God has placed us. There are times in a believer's life in which the spiritual walk becomes dim. It is through books and Bible topics such as those discussed here that we are reminded of our course in life.

Let us continue to be mindful of who we are in Christ. This is vital information! Let us not be scared or intimidated by the wiles of devil, but let us do as God called us to do - that is, to walk in heavenly authority.

To contact the author for speaking or conference engagements, send all communication to joshuaarmy11@gmail.com or via telephone at (205) 533-1707.

BIBLIOGRAPHY

"Scripture quotations taken from the Amplified®Bible, Copyright © 1987, 1965, 1964, 1962, 1958, 1954 by The Lockman Foundation, All rights reserved.

King James Version, The First Scofield Study Bible, Barbour and Company, Inc, Copyright 1986, All Rights Reserved.

Biographical Sketch of Michael A. Shine, MBA

Michael A. Shine was born in Birmingham, AL. to the proud parents of Mr. and Mrs. Mose Shine Jr. where he is the youngest of 7 children (five girls and two boys). He attend Kingston Elementary School, K-8 and attended Carol W. Hayes High School Class of 1989 (Birmingham, Alabama) and furthered his education at the University of Montevallo 1993, (Montevallo, Alabama) where he received a Bachelors of Business Administration Degree in Sales and Marketing and his MBA from Capella University in 2008. He also received his Juris Doctor of Law from Arizona Summit, 2009 (Phoenix, AZ) and Clerked at the Law firm of Bradley, Aarant Rose and White and his Ph.D. in Business Administration from Grand Canyon University in 2023. He is a member of Alpha Phi Alpha Fraternity, Inc.

On Father's of 1993, Michael preached his first sermon at First Baptist Church of East Boyles where he was licensed and ordained under the leadership of Rev. Clyde Beverly Sr. where he also served in the capacity of Youth Minister for 8 years. He attended Birmingham Easonian Bible College for 3 years.

He is currently a member of Face2Face Worship Center under the leadership of Lead Pastor, Anthony Xavier Page, Clinton, MD where her preaches and teaches small group Bible studies.

He currently owns his own Consulting and Legal firm (Shine's Professional Services, LLC)

He was dubbed by his family as the "Father of the Shine Family" as he carried out his father's wishes to promise to take care of the family, and to make sure holidays and special days were carried out. He stood by his father on his dying bed and made a vow to perform his eulogy and also took on the responsibility to be one of the main caretakers of his mother after the passing of his father on January 15, 2010.

In August 2012, Michael pursed his dream of publishing his first book entitled, "**Walking In Heavenly Authority**," where he was one of first African American writers to sell out his book at Barnes and Nobles Southern Writers' Showcase. The book is also now available on BN.Com, Amazon.com, and Books-A-Million .com and could purchase worldwide. He also Published a second one, entitled, "Excuse Me Pastor, I Don't Want Your Church!"

Michael's favorite movies are "The Color Purple" and "A River Ran Through it" and live by the Scripture, "1 Corinthians 13:12 - For now we see through a glass, darkly; but then face to face: now I know in part; but then shall I know even as also I am known."

www.ingramcontent.com/pod-product-compliance
Lightning Source LLC
LaVergne TN
LVHW061036070526
838201LV00073B/5055